FOOL PROOF

Strategies for Navigating Life God's Way

BY

ROBERT J MAXIE Sr.

Table Of Contents

DEDICATION

To the Source of Wisdom,

This book is dedicated to those who seek God's wisdom in every corner of life. From forgiveness to overcoming procrastination, may these pages be a guiding light, illuminating the path as you journey through life's intricacies.

ACKNOWLEDGMENT

I've always loved writing, and making a book now has been incredible in this part of my life. We've been blessed with a new Church building, and a new home, and our business has expanded, all thanks to God. Without God, I'm nothing – He deserves all the credit!

The Bible tells us that he who finds a wife finds a good thing, and I found the best one in my wife, Aminga. I want to thank her for pushing me to do better things, even when they're outside my comfort zone. Thanks so much for loving me, and I love you, babe. Keep believing in yourself and going after your dreams that God has promised.

I also want to thank my awesome kids – Shakira, Bobby, Kianna, Olivia, Elijah, and Jon'Benet. You've always supported me and joined in with whatever I felt God wanted me to do. You make me want to be the best dad I can be. It's amazing to see the great young men and women you've become!

To the greatest church ever – Liberty Church of Baton Rouge. You've been with me from our early days in the living room to the library, and now to our incredible new building. You've trusted me and followed me as I've grown in my faith. Thanks so much for all that you do. Let's keep moving forward and changing the world together.

Lastly, a big thanks to my publishing team, especially Emediong and the designers, and everyone who helped out. You've turned my dream into reality. I hope God blesses all beyond what you could hope or think!

And finally, to you, dear reader, I offer my heartfelt gratitude. It is through your curiosity, your hunger for understanding, and your pursuit of a life enriched by wisdom that this book finds its purpose. May you find solace, guidance, and inspiration within these pages, as together we explore the profound gift of wisdom that God has graciously bestowed upon us.

INTRODUCTION

In a world where uncertainty often looms and challenges abound, imagine possessing a secret key that guarantees success at every turn, regardless of your experience or expertise. Imagine a life where mistakes and failures become a distant memory and where a carefully crafted plan ensures your every step is guided with precision. This is the essence of the book: FOOLPROOF—a concept that transcends mere reliability to unveil a realm where success is not just probable but inevitable.

Within the pages of this transformative masterpiece, you are about to embark on a journey of revelation and empowerment. Prepare to discover that there is a divine design intricately woven into the fabric of our existence, a design that promises us safety amid turbulent waters. Just as a loving parent strategically places stones in a river to provide a safe passage, so too has the Creator bestowed upon us a foolproof strategy to navigate the currents of life.

Delve deep into the wisdom of ancient scriptures, where the voice of the divine resonates with unmistakable clarity. In the words of ***Isaiah 30:21 (ESV)***, God reassures us, ***"And your ears shall hear a word behind you, saying, 'This is the way, walk in it,' when you turn to the right or when you turn to the left."*** This promise, like a compass guiding a ship through treacherous seas, beckons us toward a life of purpose and fulfillment.

As you read and learn from the important ideas in this book, you'll feel more sure of yourself. This strong feeling will give you the courage to handle both the good and tough times in life. Armed with the radiant wisdom of God, you will rise above adversity, your path illuminated by the light of God's guidance.

CHAPTER ONE

Closet Space

"For you will save the humble people, but will bring down the haughty looks."

(Psalms 18:27 NKJV)

Within the depths of God's character lies an extraordinary quality that is both profound and beautiful—the unfathomable capacity to forgive. Throughout the timeless pages of the Old Testament and the New Testament, this remarkable trait weaves its way as a recurring theme, testifying to the boundless mercy and grace of the divine. One book, in particular, shines a light on God's readiness and eagerness to extend forgiveness to those who humbly acknowledge their need for His mercy—Isaiah. ***"Come now let us reason together, says the Lord. Though your sins are like scarlet they shall be as white as snow; though they are red as crimson, they shall be as wool." Isaiah 1:18.*** These words are an invitation to dialogue, an opportunity for reconciliation between the Creator and His creation. The imagery of scarlet turning snow-white and crimson transforming into pure wool conveys the transformative power of God's forgiveness—a complete washing away and removal of our transgressions. It is a visual representation of the restoration and purity that His forgiveness brings.

No matter how deep our transgressions may be, God's mercy surpasses them all, ready to embrace us in forgiveness. Have you ever pondered the unique attribute displayed in the life of the prophet Hosea? His remarkable experiences and walk with God serve as a vivid portrayal of the forgiving nature of our Creator. Journey with me into the book of Hosea, where an extraordinary story unfolds—a tale that illuminates the depths of God's mercy and love. In the book of Hosea, we encounter a narrative unlike any other. God, in His divine wisdom, instructs the prophet Hosea to marry a woman known for her unfaithfulness. This union between Hosea and the unfaithful woman serves as a symbolic representation of the unfaithfulness of the people of Israel toward God. Despite the pain and heartache Hosea endures, he chooses to love his unfaithful wife and remain steadfast in their relationship.

In 2 Chronicles 7:14, God tenderly instructs us on the pathway to His forgiveness. He reveals that if we humbly approach Him, offering our prayers and earnestly seeking His face, He will hear us from the depths of heaven and extend His forgiveness. The assurance of divine pardon is granted to all who come before Him with genuine humility and an open heart. Throughout the Bible, we witness a multitude of promises regarding God's forgiveness, yet often we fail to fully experience the richness of this aspect of God's character. Why? Because we approach Him with hearts filled with pride and self-righteousness. Pride blinds us to our own desperate need for forgiveness and hardens our hearts, preventing us from receiving the abundant grace available to us. In our interactions with others, we often find ourselves hesitant to be transparent, fearing their scrutiny and judgment. This fear seeps into our relationship with God as well. We hide our faults and shortcomings, concealing them in the closets of our hearts, reluctant to expose our vulnerabilities before Him. Instead, we strive to present an image of flawlessness, even to the One who sees beyond our facades.

Self-righteousness, at its core, is a refusal to submit to the righteousness of God. It is an attitude that stems from self-sufficiency and pride, distorting our perception of our righteousness and diminishing our reliance on God's grace. When we fall into the trap of self-righteousness, we believe that we can earn our salvation or merit God's favor through our efforts and good works. We become ensnared in a cycle of comparison, viewing ourselves as more righteous or deserving than others. This dangerous mindset blinds us to our need for God's forgiveness and grace. It leads us to a place of complacency in our perceived righteousness, where we fail to recognize the depth of our brokenness and our desperate need for divine mercy. In essence, self-righteousness hinders our ability to fully grasp the profound reality of God's righteousness and its transformative power in our lives. In the book of Romans, the Apostle Paul offers a prayer of great significance—one that demands our earnest consideration. Paul, acknowledging the Jews' fervor for God's work, expresses deep concern for their salvation due to their lack of understanding regarding God's righteousness. It serves as a poignant reminder for us as Christians to reflect on our understanding and attitudes concerning the righteousness of God. We must heed Paul's prayer, taking it to heart and ensuring that we do not fall into the trap of ignorance when it comes to God's righteousness. It requires a humble examination of our hearts, a willingness to release the grip of self-righteousness, and a renewed commitment to surrender to God's perfect righteousness.

Self-righteousness becomes a stumbling block when we set lofty standards for ourselves, relying solely on our capabilities to meet them. Though setting standards can be beneficial, the danger arises when we place trust in our righteousness, disregarding our inherent limitations and imperfections. When we inevitably fall short of these self-imposed standards, a cycle of self-doubt and unworthiness engulfs us. We find ourselves hesitant to approach God, for we feel tarnished and undeserving of His forgiveness. The weight of our failures erodes our confidence, leaving us uncertain of whether God's forgiveness can truly reach us. In our misguided attempt to carry on as if nothing has happened, we neglect the vital step of approaching God with humility and confessing our sins. By refusing to rest in the completed work of God's righteousness through Jesus' sacrificial offering, we limit our spiritual growth. We become overly cautious in our approach to God, lacking the confidence to honestly acknowledge our sins before Him. Instead of embracing the freedom that comes from genuine repentance and reconciliation with God, we opt for a façade of having it all together. We ignore the unresolved issues within ourselves, hoping that by pretending, we can bypass the need for true repentance.

Within the depths of our lives lie hidden closet spaces that harbor secrets, sins, and shame. These metaphorical closets represent the areas we strive to keep hidden from others, believing that as long as they remain concealed, they won't affect us or our relationship with God. We convince ourselves that by simply closing the doors to these putrefied closets and carrying on with a façade of righteousness, everything will be fine. However, the truth is far from it. When we deceive ourselves with the belief that we can keep our hidden sins locked away, we initiate a cycle of resentment and self-destruction. Just as the hypocritical Pharisees entered the temple to pray, boasting of their righteousness while harboring unconfessed sins, we too engage in a dangerous game of self-righteousness. This self-perpetuating cycle hinders our ability to experience true freedom and reconciliation. We become imprisoned by our hidden sins and the weight of unconfessed guilt. We shield ourselves from the healing power of forgiveness, both from God and from others. The walls we build around our hidden closets not only distance us from authentic relationships but also obstruct the transformative work that forgiveness can bring.

Before delving into the consequences of unconfessed sin on our ability to forgive and harbor resentment, it is vital to comprehend the spiritual destructiveness it brings to our lives. In Proverbs 28:13, God provides us with clear guidance, emphasizing that those who fail to confess their sins will not experience prosperity, but those who acknowledge and renounce their sins will receive His merciful grace. To fully grasp the significance of this verse, it is enlightening to explore the original Hebrew word used for "prosper" in Proverbs 28:13—*tsalach*. This term encompasses meanings such as "to prosper," "to have success," or "to be successful." Within the context of the verse, it refers to the positive outcome or result that arises from confessing and turning away from our sins. By neglecting to confess our sins, we hinder our ability to prosper and succeed in our relationship with God.

One of the initial signs of failure in our relationship with God is the denial of His mercies, replaced instead by His righteous condemnation. In the first chapter of the book of Isaiah, we witness the lamentable state of Israel—a once-thriving nation that had been abundantly provided for and nurtured by God. However, they have now fallen into a state of devastation, invaded by outsiders and left defenseless, akin to a besieged city. They have transitioned from experiencing the divine VIP treatment, guarded by God's jealousy, to finding themselves vulnerable and exposed. It is like moving from the safety of an impenetrable fortress to the fragility of a paper mache fort. Consider the irony of attempting to conceal our sins and guilt from the all-seeing eye of God—the One who knows us inside out. He is the God who observes our every move, from when we sit to when we rise. He even knows the very thoughts that wander through our minds, regardless of how far we may think we are. Despite this comprehensive knowledge, God desires us to humbly approach Him, confess our sins, and seek His mercy.

In Isaiah 1:11, we are confronted with a sobering truth: God was not pleased with the burnt offerings presented by the Israelites. The people mistakenly believed that these sacrifices could atone for their sins, but they were gravely mistaken. Rather than opening their hearts to God, confessing their wrongdoings, and seeking His forgiveness, they persisted in performing empty rituals. This deeply disappointed God, leading Him to withdraw His mercy from them. Their lack of true remorse and genuine repentance hindered the restoration of their relationship with Him. The Israelites' misguided belief that mere external actions could compensate for their sins highlights a fundamental misunderstanding of God's desires. God longs for more than empty rituals or superficial gestures of devotion. He desires heartfelt sincerity and genuine repentance from His people. In their failure to embrace genuine repentance, the Israelites missed the opportunity for true restoration and reconciliation with God. Their empty rituals lacked the substance needed to bridge the gap between their sinful nature and God's righteousness. The consequence was the withdrawal of God's mercy, leaving them in a state of spiritual desolation.

Living without the mercies of God leaves us vulnerable to the whims and caprices of the devil—an existence akin to entering an intense battlefield without any armor. It is imperative to establish the fact that when we lack transparency in our relationship with God, we miss out on experiencing His abundant mercies. In the New Testament, the Apostle Paul delineates the spiritual weapons necessary for the believer's triumph in spiritual warfare. In Ephesians 6, Paul describes salvation as a helmet—an essential piece of armor in warfare. Imagine the grave consequences if we were to lose this helmet by concealing our sins. The attacks we would face would be overwhelming and devastating. It is a perilous state to find oneself in. The devil, as explained in 1 Peter 5:8, is often depicted as a roaring lion seeking someone to devour. He exploits our weaknesses and capitalizes on our lack of spiritual defenses. When we disregard or neglect God's mercies, we unwittingly expose ourselves to his cunning tactics. The absence of divine protection leaves us defenseless and vulnerable to the enemy's schemes. The armor of God, outlined by Paul, equips us to withstand and overcome the onslaughts of the enemy. Each piece of this spiritual armor—the belt of truth, the breastplate of righteousness, the readiness of the gospel of peace, the shield of faith, the helmet of salvation, and the sword of the Spirit—plays a vital role in our defense against the devil's tactics.

The devil takes pleasure in inflicting wounds on our souls, seeking to rob us of the peace, joy, and spiritual well-being that God desires for us. Throughout the pages of the Bible, the devil is depicted as a cunning and relentless adversary, identified as the father of lies, as stated in John 8:44; the accuser of the brethren, Revelation 12:10; and the tempter who seeks to deceive, Matthew 4:3. His ultimate aim is to sever our connection with God and hinder our relationship with Him. A pivotal moment in human history illustrates the devil's tactics. When Adam and Eve succumbed to his deception and partook of the forbidden fruit, they experienced a profound shift. Suddenly, they became acutely aware of their nakedness, which filled them with shame. Instead of embracing vulnerability and openness before God, they chose to hide among the trees of the garden, attempting to conceal themselves. This marked the onset of their broken relationship with God. The devil's strategy is to exploit our vulnerabilities and sow seeds of doubt and deception. He tempts us with empty promises, distorts the truth, and capitalizes on our weaknesses. His primary objective is to separate us from God, convincing us that we are unworthy of His love and forgiveness.

It is intriguing to contemplate the potential outcome if Adam and Eve had taken a different approach after their fall in the Garden of Eden. Instead of hiding and attempting to conceal their actions, what if they had humbly approached God, openly confessing their deception by the serpent and their disobedience? Surely, God's response would have been one of mercy and forgiveness. In ***Psalms 32:5 (BBE)***, David expresses his own experience of confessing his wrongdoing to God: ***"I made my wrongdoing clear to you and did not keep back my sin. I said, I will put it all before the Lord, and you took away my wrongdoing and my sin."*** This passage reveals the power of repentance and the boundless mercy of God. Had Adam and Eve chosen to approach God with genuine repentance, acknowledging their transgressions and seeking His forgiveness, it is reasonable to believe that God would have shown them the same mercy He demonstrated to David. God is a loving and compassionate Father, eager to extend forgiveness to those who genuinely repent and turn to Him. By confessing their sins and seeking God's forgiveness, Adam and Eve would have opened the door to restoration. They would have initiated a process of reconciliation, allowing God to cleanse and renew their hearts. Through their humility and repentance, they would have received the fullness of God's mercy, experiencing the healing and restoration of their relationship with Him. Reflecting on this possibility emphasizes the transformative power of repentance and the unending depth of God's mercy. It serves as a reminder for us that no matter how deep our failures or how grievous our sins are, God is always ready to extend His forgiveness and restore us to a place of fellowship with Him.

The mercy of God stands as a shield, protecting us from being consumed by the works of Satan. Each day, His mercies are renewed, a testament to His unending love and compassion toward us. It is crucial to acknowledge that any unfaithfulness we encounter in our lives does not originate from God. Instead, it arises from our own choices and actions. God, on the other hand, is consistently faithful, and His mercies know no bounds.

Dangers of Hiding Our Sins and Struggles in Our Closet Spaces

1. Resentment

As we have established, if we stubbornly refuse to open our hearts to God and allow Him to cleanse us with His purifying love, we will find ourselves trapped in a cycle of resentment. The story of Peter and John encountering the crippled man at the Beautiful Gate in the Book of Acts serves as a poignant example of the principle that we can only give what we possess. As the Apostles approached the temple for prayer, the man, who had been crippled from birth, sought financial assistance from them. Expecting to receive silver or gold, he looked at them with hopeful eyes. Peter's response to the man resonates with the truth that one cannot give what one does not possess. He acknowledged that he did not possess material wealth in the form of silver or gold. However, he recognized that he had something far more powerful to offer—the name of Jesus Christ of Nazareth. In faith, Peter extended the healing power of Jesus' name, commanding the man to rise and walk. Miraculously, the man's crippled legs were restored, and he experienced the transformative power of God's love.

Many of us find ourselves trapped in the prison of resentment and unforgiveness because we have neglected to confess our sins and receive the boundless mercy and forgiveness that God offers. Without personally experiencing God's mercy and forgiveness, we struggle to extend forgiveness to others. However, forgiveness is deeply rooted in love. To grasp the true essence of forgiveness, let us turn our attention to ***Ephesians 2:4.*** This verse illuminates the nature of God's forgiveness, stating, ***"But***

God, who is rich in mercy, is rich in mercy because of the great love with which He loved us." Here, we encounter the profound truth that God's mercy toward us is an outpouring of His immeasurable love. His mercy, which leads to the forgiveness of our sins, is a tangible expression of the overwhelming love He has for us. God's forgiveness is not a detached act; it is intimately intertwined with His love. It is through His love that He extends mercy, erasing the stains of our transgressions and offering us a fresh start. His forgiveness is a reflection of His deep desire to restore and reconcile us to Himself. In the upcoming chapters, we will delve into the concept of forgiveness, exploring its nuances and implications. We will examine how forgiveness flows from God's mercy and love, and how it has the power to set us free from the chains of resentment and unforgiveness. Through this exploration, we will uncover the transformative nature of forgiveness and discover practical steps toward embracing its healing power.

2. Emotional Burden

Hiding our struggles and sins burdens us emotionally, weighing us down with guilt. In ***Psalms 38:4***, David vividly expresses the overwhelming nature of this burden, stating, ***"My guilt overwhelms me—it is a burden too heavy to bear" (NLT).*** When we conceal our guilt, it intensifies, becoming a weight too difficult to carry. This burden stifles our joy, robs us of peace, and inhibits our freedom. The longer we hold onto guilt, the more it consumes us, impacting our thoughts, emotions, and overall mental well-being. The book of Lamentations illustrates the anguish of Jerusalem as she laments the consequences of her rebellion against God. ***Lamentations 1:20*** conveys the brokenness of the heart and despair of the soul resulting from rebellion: ***"Lord, see my anguish! My heart is broken, and my soul despairs, for I have rebelled against you."*** In her book "Start Your New Life," Joyce Meyer astutely points out that guilt is the constant companion of sinners. It is the heavy emotional burden we bear when we choose to cover up our sins. This guilt weighs us down, convincing us that we are unworthy of God's blessings and forgiveness. If left unchecked, this burden becomes fertile ground through which the devil exploits us and wreaks havoc in our lives. The key to liberation lies in confronting and releasing the hidden guilt within us. We must recognize that God's desire is not to condemn us but to offer us forgiveness, healing, and restoration. It is through acknowledging our sins, confessing them before God, and seeking His forgiveness that we can experience the freedom and lightness of a burden lifted. When we open ourselves to God's mercy, confessing our sins with humility and repentance, His forgiveness washes over us, purifying our hearts and restoring our souls. We find solace in His boundless love and grace, and the heavy burden of hidden guilt is transformed into a source of renewal and transformation.

3. Physical Deterioration

David's experience of committing adultery with Bathsheba and orchestrating Uriah's murder stands as a powerful example of the devastating consequences of unconfessed sins. In ***Psalms 32:3-4(NKJV) "When I kept silent, my bones grew old through my groaning all day long. For day***

and night, Your hand was heavy upon me; My vitality was turned into the drought of summer. Selah," David candidly expresses the toll that his hidden sins took on his physical and emotional well-being. He describes how his "bones grew old" and his vitality turned into the drought of summer because he did not confess his sins. The weight of unconfessed sins can have a profound impact on our lives. It gnaws at our conscience, draining us of joy and vitality. Just as David experienced the deterioration of his physical and emotional state, unconfessed sins can lead to a spiritual drought, leaving us parched and disconnected from the abundant life God desires for us. When we choose to conceal our sins, we bear the weight of guilt and shame alone. We become entangled in a web of lies, attempting to cover up our transgressions. The longer we hide, the deeper the despair and desolation we experience. In ***Psalms 32:5***, he declares, ***"I acknowledged my sin to you, and I did not cover my iniquity; I said, 'I will confess my transgressions to the Lord,' and you forgave the iniquity of my sin."***

When we are silent about our sinful struggles and acts, we open up our physical health to sickness. The correlation between repentance and healing is a powerful truth that resonates throughout Scripture. David's lament in Psalm 38 reflects the consequences of his sins, as he expresses that there is no soundness in his flesh and no health in his bones. His physical afflictions serve as a poignant reminder that silence about our sinful struggles and acts can impact our physical health. In the book of 2 Chronicles, God makes a profound promise to His people. If they humble themselves, pray, seek His face, and turn away from their wicked ways, He will hear their prayers and heal their land. This promise demonstrates the interconnectedness of repentance, prayer, and healing. It emphasizes that our spiritual posture has a direct impact on our physical well-being. The account of the paralytic brought before Jesus in Capernaum further underscores the connection between sin, forgiveness, and healing. When the paralytic was brought to Jesus, Jesus proclaimed, "Son, your sins are forgiven you." While his friends had brought him with the intention of physical healing, Jesus prioritized the forgiveness of his sins. This highlights the profound understanding that sin, rebellion, and the unwillingness to open up and forsake our sins can have far-reaching consequences that extend beyond the spiritual realm.

The entrance of sin into the world through the disobedience of Adam and Eve resulted in a brokenness that affected every aspect of human existence. The consequences of sin can manifest in various forms, including physical sickness and affliction. However, the healing power of God is not limited to the physical realm alone. It encompasses the restoration of our whole being—spirit, soul, and body. When we humble ourselves, repent, and seek God's forgiveness, we invite His healing touch into every area of our lives. As we turn away from our wicked ways and open ourselves to God's transforming grace, we position ourselves for restoration and wholeness. The forgiveness of our sins, through the redemptive work of Jesus Christ, becomes a gateway to experiencing the healing and restoration that God desires for us.

4. Spiritual Stuntedness And Death

The violation of God's commandment by Adam and Eve in the Garden of Eden had grave consequences. They were driven out of the Garden, separated from God's presence, and barred from eating from the Tree of Life, which would have granted them eternal life. It is important to understand that God's intention was never to prevent Adam and Eve from living forever but rather to ensure that they would not live forever in a sinful state. God's desire has always been for humanity to have dominion and to reign with Him eternally. Jesus affirmed this in the New Testament, declaring that He came to give us life in abundance. However, living forever with a sinful nature is incompatible with the holiness of God. Sin creates enmity between us and God. He is holy, and He can only intimately dwell with those who have accepted His gift of righteousness and holiness.

In *1 Peter 1:15–16*, Apostle Peter exhorts believers to be holy in all their conduct, for it is written, "***You shall be holy, for I am holy.***" Adam and Eve, by partaking in the Tree of

Knowledge of Good and Evil, embraced the nature of sin. In their sinful state, they could not remain in the presence of a holy God, and thus they were separated from Him. The consequences of this separation are profound. When we are disconnected from God, we cease to abide in the vine. We become like withered branches, spiritually stunted and unable to bear the fruit that God intended for us. The separation from God marks the beginning of spiritual decay, ultimately leading to spiritual and physical death, yet even amid this separation, God's redemptive plan is set in motion. He desires to restore us to a place of intimacy and communion with Him. Through the sacrifice of Jesus Christ, God provided the means for reconciliation. Through faith in Christ and accepting His gift of righteousness, we are brought back into a restored relationship with God.

In 2 Peter 3:9, we are reminded of God's deep desire for all people to come to repentance and be saved. God's heart is not for anyone to perish but for all to experience His forgiveness and restoration. Understanding this truth, it becomes evident that harboring unconfessed sins while actively serving God in the church is futile. The cautionary tale of Ananias and Sapphira serves as a stark reminder of the consequences of hiding unconfessed sins from the Holy Spirit. Their story is one of missed blessings and tragic outcomes, as they willfully chose to deceive and withhold the truth before the presence of God. Their refusal to be open and transparent resulted in dire consequences.

In all things, there is hope. The assurance is found in ***1 John 1:9,*** which states, ***"If we confess our sins, He is faithful and just to forgive us our sins and to cleanse us from all unrighteousness."*** God's faithfulness and justice are evident when we humbly confess our sins before Him. He is ready and eager to forgive us, wash away our sins, and restore us to a place of righteousness and purity. Repentance is the key that unlocks the door to God's forgiveness and cleansing. It is the turning away from our sinful ways and the surrendering of our hearts to His transformative grace. When we confess our sins, we open ourselves to the transformative work of God's forgiveness, experiencing the freedom, joy, and restoration that come with it. Let us not deceive ourselves by trying to hide our sins or by serving God with unconfessed transgressions in our hearts. Instead, let us humbly approach God, acknowledging our need for His forgiveness and mercy. Through repentance, we can walk in the light of His truth, fully embracing the blessings and abundant life He has prepared for us. As we embark on the journey of repentance and confession, let us remember that God desires to cleanse us, restore us, and draw us closer to Him. Let us lay aside the weight of unconfessed sins, embracing the freedom and joy that come from a sincere and repentant heart. In doing so, we will experience the fullness of God's forgiveness, His blessings, and the richness of a life transformed by His grace.

CHAPTER TWO

Never Scared

"Trust in the Lord with all your heart and lean not on your own understanding"

(Proverbs 3:5 NKJV)

In the journey of a truly victorious Christian life, there lies a profound essence—a complete surrender to the divine. It is the deliberate release of our own will, desires, and apprehensions, allowing us to embrace the unfathomable will, promises, commandments, and perfect timing of God. This embodiment of childlike faith and audacious surrender is precisely what our Heavenly Father yearns for in His faithful followers—a "never scared" attitude that rests completely on His ordained plans for our lives.

One obstacle that prevents us from embracing the magnificent plans that God has designed for us is fear. When fear is mentioned, we often envision someone trapped in a dim prison cell, paralyzed with fright, unable to venture into the magnificent and freeing world that God has prepared for them. Their thoughts become a breeding ground for desolate and disheartening ideas, making it increasingly challenging to trust in a promising future. However, fear also manifests when a young woman clings to a bouquet of artificial flowers. These flowers may appear vivid and captivating, but they lack the genuine aroma and vitality that real flowers provide.

The Nature of Fear

Fear is a cunning weapon that the devil employs to cripple our lives. He sows seeds of doubt and fear, seeking to undermine the assurance we have in the Word of God. Yet, it is the Word of God that we can trust to bring forth the reality we desire and dismantle that which is destructive in our lives. When God speaks concerning our situations, He releases a powerful remedy capable of transforming our circumstances. His words are like capsules of divine provision and guidance. However, we must actively receive and allow His words to take effect in our lives. It is through faith and obedience that we unlock the full potential of His promises. A powerful example of overcoming fear through faith is found in the transition of leadership from Moses to Joshua. After Moses's death, the responsibility of leading the Israelites fell upon Joshua. Leading the people after the mighty leader Moses was no small burden, requiring unwavering faith in the assurance of God's promises. God's words to Joshua provided the strength and encouragement he needed to step into his leadership role with confidence. In ***Joshua 1:9,*** God said, ***"Have I not commanded you? Be strong and courageous. Do not be afraid; do not be discouraged, for the Lord your God will be with you wherever you go."*** These words became a beacon of hope and a source of assurance for Joshua as he faced the challenges before him.

When Joshua took on the mantle of leadership, God made astounding promises to him. He assured Joshua of complete dominion over the surrounding territories and promised to manifest Himself as a mighty man of valor during their battles. God guaranteed that no man would be able to defeat Joshua throughout his lifetime. It may seem that with such remarkable promises, nothing more needs to be said. However, God sternly warned Joshua to expel fear from his life. Fear has a profound impact on our perception of God and can hinder us from fully experiencing His power and authority. It distorts our view of His faithfulness and can lead us to doubt His ability to fulfill His promises. When fear takes root in our hearts, it hinders our faith and limits our capacity to walk in the fullness of what God has in store for us.

Fear often arises when we find ourselves in situations where we lack a sense of control. When we become acutely aware of our limited ability to influence or determine the outcome of a particular circumstance we get gripped with fear. As humans, we are wired naturally to desire stability and security. So, when faced with circumstances that challenge our security and stability, we begin to amplify "what-ifs" scenarios and worst-case possibilities over the safety of the promises of God.

The Israelites' journey from slavery in Egypt to the Promised Land is a powerful example of the human struggle with fear and faith. Their lives were filled with unbearable hardships under the oppressive rule of Pharaoh. Forced to work tirelessly and face heartless overseers, they endured physical exhaustion and unimaginable challenges daily. In their desperation, they cried out to God, and He heard their cries. Through mighty acts of deliverance, God freed them from the grip of their oppressors and demonstrated His power and faithfulness. They witnessed firsthand the miracles of God, from the plagues that humiliated the Egyptians to the parting of the Red Sea, which allowed them to walk through on dry ground. With these powerful experiences of God's salvation, one would expect their faith to be firm and unwavering. God had promised to lead them to the land He had promised their fathers, assuring them of His presence throughout their journey. However, when they faced challenges and hardships in the wilderness, their faith wavered, and fear began to take hold. The Israelites became consumed by their immediate struggles, forgetting the love and faithfulness of God. They lost sight of His miraculous deliverance and allowed fear to overshadow His promises. Instead of trusting in God's guidance, they succumbed to doubt and complained against Him.

Fear has a powerful way of limiting our perspective and distorting our perception of God's promises. When we allow fear to take hold of us, we become jittery and frightened, and our words and actions contradict the truths recorded in the Bible. In our desperate search for comfort, we start to believe the facts of our situation, which often seem far from the truth of God's promises. The Israelites' journey through the wilderness serves as a vivid example of the destructive nature of fear. Despite witnessing the mighty acts of God's deliverance from the oppressive rule of Pharaoh, they allowed their state of misery to overshadow the assurance God had given them regarding their journey to the promised land. In their desperation, they began to long for death and murmured bitterly against Moses and Aaron. In their fear, the Israelites seemed to have hastily discarded the memory of God's strength and capabilities. They forgot how He had acted as a warrior, overthrowing Pharaoh's chariots and parting the Red Sea to fulfill His promise. Instead of clinging to the truth of God's power and faithfulness, they spoke words that made God angry and hindered their progress.

In Exodus chapter 16, these people began to orchestrate their death. The words they uttered were a stark contrast to the assurance they had from God. They told Moses that it was better they died in Egypt where they had access to satisfactory meals rather than starve to death in the wilderness. Fear had caused them to reprogram their destinies negatively. Instead of declaring strength in their moment of weakness, they desired death.

Fear makes you lose sight. When you lose sight and consciousness of the authority God has bestowed on you, you lose your sound mind and wander into the abyss of darkness. When your mind is clouded, the Chief of

Darkness uses that opportunity to guide you onto doom by affecting your utterances negatively Our words are the powerful tools of warfare we have. If we speak the truth – the word of God that is Yes and Amen, throughout all generations, we win over the devil. It may not look like we're winning immediately, but those words are clearing up the paths to our victory. The Bible says in ***Joel 3:10, "Let the weak say I am strong"***. When we study the context of Joel chapter three, we see that the setting here is a war front. In a season of fierce battle, God calls on the nation of Judah and the entire Jerusalem to put on their garments of war. He speaks to the mighty men and commands them to be ready to attack. Not only does he invite the best men of war, but he also recruits the weak. What army general will look for the weakest of men to deploy to the war front? I do not know of any. But God does. He extends an invitation to the weak and commands them to believe that they are strong. Wait! This story sounds familiar. Do you remember Gideon?

The nation of Israel had yet again been taken under captivity by the Midianites for seven years because of their disobedience to God. The Midianites attacked their farm produce and would take everything they planted during the season of harvest. They also attacked their animals and destroyed their lands. The Israelites lived in constant hiding to preserve the little they had. This was the situation Gideon was in when the Angel of the Lord met him. He was ***"threshing wheat at the bottom of the winepress to hide the grain from the Midianite" (Judges 6:11b, NLT).***

Gideon was weak and powerless, yet the Angel of God addressed him as a ***"mighty man of valor."*** That statement must have bewildered Gideon. A mighty man of valor secretly beats the wheat at the bottom of the winepress instead of doing that in an open field just to hide from his enemies. Isn't a mighty man of valor entrusted with the responsibility of fighting off encroachers from his territory? After the Lord had spelled out Gideon's calling to save Israel from the hand of the Midianites, he expressed fear. Gideon was from the least clan in Manasseh and also the least in his clan. He was the last of the least; unknown and insignificant. The Lord nibbed that seed of fear in the bud. He said to him

"Surely I will be with you, and you shall defeat the Midianites as one man." Gideon chose to believe the word of God over his family and societal status. It was true that he had no influence in His clan and was completely insignificant in his own family, and those were valid fears and concerns when considering the eligibility of the person who would deliver the Israelites from the Midianites. How could someone who held no sway within his clan or family possibly rise to lead a nation in battle? But, God's word had gone ahead of him and It carried a weight and power far greater than any earthly influence or status. But it was not only God's word that made the difference. Gideon himself had a crucial role to play. He had a choice to make. He could either allow fear to cripple him, or he could embrace the word of God and step into a completely new experience. Fortunately, Gideon allowed the word of God to dissipate his fears.

When God calls us to step out of our comfort zones, embark on new journeys, or face challenges of great magnitude, fear, and anxiety often arise within us. In those moments, we may temporarily forget the countless times we have witnessed the mighty hand of God at work in our lives. Fear overshadows our trust in God, causing us to doubt His ability to continue working wonders on our behalf. As human beings, we are prone to forgetfulness. We easily lose sight of God's faithfulness and the incredible works He has done on our behalf. In our moments of fear and doubt, we may neglect to remember the times He delivered us, provided for us, and guided us through difficult circumstances. Throughout the Bible, we see that God repeatedly urges His people to remember His commandments, His promises, and His goodness. Let's look at what God says in ***Deuteronomy 4:9, "Only give heed to yourself and keep your soul diligently so that you do not forget the things which your eyes have seen and they do not depart from your heart all the days of your life, but make them known to your sons and your grandsons."***

God emphasizes the importance of keeping His words and commandments before us at all times. When He instructs us to keep our soul diligently, He understands that our spirit is already aligned with the reality of the Spirit, but our soul—

the mind, will, and emotions—needs to catch up. Our spirit is confident in relying completely on God because the Spirit of God bears witness to our spirit that we are His children. As His children, we have a part in His inheritance, which grants us access to divine health, prosperity, success, and dominion. Our spirit is already assured of all the blessings we have in Jesus Christ. However, our soul often struggles to grasp this truth. Our soul is easily influenced by our physical experiences and realities, leading to doubt, fear, and unbelief. It is in the realm of the soul that we wrestle with the discrepancy between our current circumstances and the promises of God.

Keeping our souls diligently means brooding over the word of God all day long so they become a hedge that dispels fear. When we discipline our souls to brood, think, ponder, stay long, and be influenced by the Word of God, we develop a strong foundation of truth. The truth sets us free from the destructive claws of fear and helps us shift our focus from the temporary and fleeting circumstances of this world to the eternal and unchanging promises of God. Let us commit to keeping our soul diligently, knowing that by doing so, we position ourselves to fully embrace the abundant life that God has prepared for us. May our minds be transformed, our wills surrendered, and our emotions guided by the truth of His word. In doing so, we walk in the fullness of our identity as children of God, confidently embracing His promises and living out His purposes for our lives.

Is God Truly With Us?

When you are in the middle of life's challenges and difficulties; trapped in a messy web of toxic relationships or dealing with the loss of an only child, you may find yourself questioning the essence of living, gripped with the fear of the unknown, and doubting the existence of God. You may be faced with a daunting medical report that contradicts the healing promised by God in Christ and your body, in its physical state, is a clear depiction of the diagnosis of the doctor, you're feeling severe pains and wondering if truly God can save you. The fear of death grips you completely, provoking a torrent of questions within your heart: Is God present? Does He truly care? Will He heal and restore my body? Or will I succumb to this ailment and face death?

After the Angel of the Lord appeared unto Gideon, he said to him, ***"The Lord is with you, you mighty man of valor."*** Gideon, in disbelief and understandably so, struggled to comprehend the weight of these words. He was part of a nation that had been reduced to nothing, dominated, and trampled upon by its enemies. They had experienced countless defeats and were now living in a state of enslavement. How could God possibly be with them when their reality seemed so bleak and pitiful? Similar to Gideon, as we observe the state of the world around us, with its chaos, wars, depression, and rampant violence, it's easy to succumb to the belief that God has abandoned us to our fate. Each morning, the news headlines assault our senses, sending shockwaves down our nerves and casting a dark cloud over our entire day. The constant barrage of distressing information leaves us feeling sick and tired. Each day brings a fresh wave of tragedies, conflicts, unsettling news, and injustices that plague our world. The world appears to be spiraling out of control and the weight of all these tribulations settles heavily in our minds. We have questions we are too broken to ask hence we just resign to fear and fate.

There are two things I want you to be settled on: The first truth is that we are not the first generation to be plagued by endless persecution and misery. The second and very important truth we must understand and believe is that God is with us. Amidst the blaring horns of pain and heartbreak that leave us gasping for air, God is with us. In the Second Corinthians chapter one from verse three, we are assured that God is the "Father of mercies, and God of all comfort, who comforts us in all our tribulations…" He is here with us and not just like a dummy who observes and is incapable of doing anything, He can comfort us in our tribulations. God does not expect us to be overwhelmed by fear like unbelievers and begin to act irrationally. He certainly abhors us uttering words of unbelief and rage when we are faced with unspeakable life circumstances. His dealing with us is for us to come to the conviction that He will never leave us nor forsake us.

The early Apostles all had an "excellent" taste of adversity because of their solid pledge to follow Jesus Christ and uphold the Gospel. After rebuking and delivering a slave girl who was possessed by the Spirit of divination, Paul and Silas were taken to the authorities of the Romans by the masters of the slave girl. They were intensely angered as they had been profiting from her fortune-telling abilities. Paul and Silas were stripped of their clothes, severely beaten with rods, and thrown into prison. If they were people who had no solid conviction in God, your guess is as good as mine. It would have been easier to deny God out of fear and save themselves the uncertainty of freedom or liberty, death or life.

We will never be able to break out of the crippling power of fear if we are not convicted of our convictions. If we do not know and are fully persuaded that God will be with us even when we walk through the valley of the shadow of death, we will never dare to venture through those valleys. Even if it means that more souls could be brought into the kingdom of God, our fear will hold us from fulfilling our purpose and carrying out the work entrusted to us. As long as we are still in this world we will inevitably face hatred, persecution, and a couple of really sad circumstances. We must have a revelation of God as ***Emmanuel*** – God with us. This is our guarantee to navigate challenges knowing that we are not alone. In Isaiah 41:10, God *commands* us to fear not for He is with us. A little child's worries quickly fade away when they realize that their loving and watchful parents are right there beside them. They feel a deep sense of security and peace knowing that no matter what challenges or dangers may arise, their parents can soothe their anxious hearts. God with us the hope of Glory, the calm to our anxious hearts, and our fortress in a fleeting world.

Different Kinds of Fear and the Limitation on our Christian Experience

1. The Fear Of Our Insufficiencies

A certain priest was struck dumb as a result of his attempt to limit God's ability to fulfill His prophetic promise. This happened because he expressed fear and doubt regarding his insufficiency. Zacharias was testified of as a righteous man who walked in all the commandments and ordinances of the Lord. He was considered blameless before God. Such zeal and testimony of perfection! At a glance, we can appreciate the commitment and reverence Zacharias had for God. One day it was his order to burn incense in the temple, and as he went in to observe his priestly ritual, he had an encounter with Angel Gabriel. Zacharias and his wife, Elizabeth were barren and were both advanced in age. He was convinced that it would be impossible for them to have any children so he questioned the message he received from Angel Gabriel. It's very fascinating to note that this was the long-awaited answer to their prayers. He almost missed it because he thought their bodies were aged and incapable of conceiving a child. When we allow the fear of our shortcomings and insufficiencies to consume us, we run the risk of missing out on experiencing the full manifestation of God's prophecies and promises in our lives. This fear becomes a stumbling block that hinders us from stepping into the abundant blessings and breakthroughs that God has prepared for us. We have to realize that it is those who answer the call of God that He glorifies. Sadly, many of us miss out on experiencing the glorious manifestation of God in our lives. Why? Because the fear of our insufficiencies engulfs us, holding us back from stepping out in faith. We convince ourselves that we are not qualified or equipped enough to fulfill God's calling.

There is something God desires to furnish in our hearts; It is the need for us to be completely detached from relying on our strengths and weaknesses, and instead, to place our full trust in Him. Often, we find ourselves relying on our abilities, talents, and achievements. We take pride in our strengths and accomplishments, believing that they are what will carry us through life's challenges. At the same time, we are all too aware of our weaknesses and shortcomings and become scared to act on what God has placed in our hearts. He desires to be our ultimate source of strength, wisdom, and guidance. God wants us to trust Him fully, leaning not on our understanding but acknowledging Him in all our ways. When we rely on our strength or allow the fear of our insufficiencies to hold us back, we miss out on the incredible journey of faith and the opportunity to witness the glory of God working through us.

2. The Fear of Failure/Past Failures

Fear of failure is a common stumbling block that hinders many from stepping into the will of God. We worry about making mistakes and falling short of expectations. We allow the fear of failure to keep us trapped in a cycle of inaction and prevent us from fully embracing the plans and purposes God has for our lives. Additionally, past failures can have a powerful hold on us. We may carry the weight of regret, guilt, and shame, allowing these experiences to define our present and limit our future. God has given us the free will to decide not to replay the memories of past failures over and over again in our minds. We are not destined to fail or fail again. Let's learn a valuable lesson from the disciples of Jesus Christ. The first and second missions God entrusted them with they went in the name of the Lord and recorded tremendous success. In ***Luke 10:17,*** they returned radiant with joy saying, ***"Lord, even the demons are subject to us in your name".*** Now, shortly after that, a man had sent his epileptic son to be healed by Jesus' disciples and they were unable to heal him. Despite their unsuccessful attempts to heal the epileptic boy, the disciples did not allow the fear of failure to deter them from seeking answers. Instead of giving up or refusing to try again, they approached Jesus with humility and asked Him questions for further understanding. Many of us would have been tempted to doubt the call and power of God in our lives and be hesitant to pray for the sick.

To free ourselves from the heavy burden of the fear of failure, we must let go of self-reliance and place our trust in God alone. When we rely solely on our abilities and strengths we become afraid of failure because we understand that our human limitations and imperfections can lead to mistakes and setbacks. Psalms 73:26 opens our eyes to the fact that our flesh and heart are prone to weakness and failure but God is the strength of our heart. However, when we shift our focus from ourselves to God, our perspective changes. We begin to realize that God has called us to remember no more the things of old. He has called us to release the weight of past mistakes, failures, and regrets.

We escape this fear of failure and past failure when we fortify our hearts with the word of God. The word of God not only dispels fear, doubt, and insecurity, but it points us to the plan of God that was written concerning us, even before we were conceived. By consistently studying and meditating on the Word of God, we align our hearts and minds with His truth. We begin to see ourselves through His eyes and understand that our worth and identity are rooted in Him, not in our past failures or perceived shortcomings. A lady who may have been through severe bitter and toxic relationships should not have a heart hardened against the possibility of being blessed with a beautiful marriage. This confidence is not just some new age mind thing, but a firm confidence rooted in the word of God in ***Isaiah 62:4 "You shall no longer be termed forsaken, Nor shall your land any more be termed desolate, but you shall be called Hephzibah, and your land Beulah; For the Lord delights in you, and your land shall be married."*** When we surrender our ways and plans to God and trust wholly in Him, we can be sure of His perfection and this gives us the confidence to step out with courage.

3. Fear of Rejection.

The fear of rejection is behind our insatiable desire to please people and care so much about their opinions. It stems from a natural human need for acceptance and belonging. However, when this fear takes hold of us, it can lead to unhealthy patterns of behavior and a constant striving for validation. We begin to conform to the perceptions and expectations of other people rather than Christ. In studying the instances when Jesus faced heavy criticism from the

Pharisees and scribes, we see a consistent pattern in His response. Rather than compromising His values and convictions to appease them or gain their approval, Jesus made it clear that He came from above, from the Father in heaven. He always emphasized His authority and superiority over them. He prioritized speaking the truth over watering down His message to appease the Pharisees and the scribes. His focus was on fulfilling His purpose and revealing the kingdom of God to humanity. Since God lives in us and made us sit with Jesus in heavenly places (Ephesians 2:6) and has given us the mandate to grow the kingdom and be Christlike, why are we still afraid of rejection? Why are we caught in the culture of conformity and acceptance based on societal standards?

If we forget that our true identity is that we are the children of God, loved and accepted by Him; If we forget that we are not called to ***"be afraid of their faces" (Jer 1:8)***, we will be consumed with the fear of rejection. I will not tell you that you will always be accepted. Jesus told us clearly in John 15:18, that the world hated Him and will surely hate us. We are not called to fear people's opinions but rather to speak and do whatever God has commanded us.

We overcome the fear of rejection by understanding our identity in God and walking in His will. If we are convinced that God has called us to a purpose, he will open up the hearts of people who are instrumental to the success of that mission. We know from the scriptures that the hearts of men are in the hands of God, and he turns them about as He wishes.

How to Overcome Fear

In my journey through ministry, I have been privileged to witness the remarkable lives of men and women of God. These individuals have weathered the storms of war, endured the painful struggles of racism, and experienced the heartbreak of losing loved ones. Despite the weariness and physical pain they have faced, I have seen their unwavering faith and fearlessness in holding onto the horn of their prayer altars. The lives of these faithful believers serve as a testament to the resilience of faith in the face of adversity. They have walked through fiery trials and emerged stronger; their confidence in God has deepened with each setback and heartbreak.

Their faith did not exempt them from the challenges of life. They faced trials like anyone else, yet they demonstrated remarkable courage and steadfastness, never allowing fear to dictate their actions or shake their faith. Their strength did not come from their abilities or human determination. Instead, it stemmed from their unshakeable trust in God and His promises. They understood that God was with them in every season of life, guiding and sustaining them. These men and women found solace in their prayer altars, where they poured out their hearts to God and sought His guidance and strength. They knew the power of prayer and relied on it as a lifeline in times of trouble. Their lives were and are still a testament to ***Psalms 37:25* "*I have been young, and now am old, Yet I have not seen the righteous forsaken, nor his descendants begging bread.*"** I consider myself incredibly privileged to have had the opportunity to meet and interact with the saints whose hearts were fully immersed in the fear and reverence of God.

In this era, the fear of God no longer reigns in the hearts of many. We have adopted a selfish posture toward our relationship with Him, seeking Him only when we desire to receive something from Him. The true value and significance of prayer have been overlooked and underestimated. For many, prayer has become a reactive response—a plea for help when everything seems to be falling apart. We approach God out of desperation, seeking His intervention to rescue us from the messes we find ourselves in, often caused by our disobedience. Instead of seeking God first, we relegate Him to a last resort when all other options have failed. Our prayers have become focused on the problems we face and the attacks of the enemy, rather than on the greatness and victory of our God, who has already defeated the enemy. We have become a generation more fearful of the devil's attacks than reverent and obedient to God. We compromise our obedience to seek acceptance in society rather than fearing and honoring the One who holds our destiny.

In Proverbs 8:13, we see that ***"the fear of the Lord is to hate evil..."*** Growing up, I had a healthy respect and reverence for my parents, which some might describe as "fear." However, it wasn't a fear that caused me to be afraid of them, but rather a recognition that they deeply loved me and had certain guidelines and expectations for my well-being. As a child, I may not have fully understood the reasons behind their standards, but I knew that they were intended to keep me safe, and healthy, and help me grow into a responsible adult. At times, in my limited understanding, it may have seemed like they were trying to hinder my fun and prevent me from getting my way. Similarly, many individuals struggle to comprehend what it truly means to "fear the Lord." This concept can be challenging to grasp because it is not about being terrified or living in constant fear of punishment.

The fear of God is a reverence and deep respect for His holiness and authority. It is the recognition that God is sovereign, wise, and just and that His will and ways are far superior to our own. It is a commitment to submit to the will of God. The Bible never lies, God assured us that the ***"righteous will be as bold as a lion" (Proverbs 28:1b).*** When our hearts are filled with the fear of God, we walk in righteousness and obedience. We are guided by His Word and Spirit, and we live in alignment with God's desire for us. This righteousness gives us confidence and boldness, knowing that we are on the path that pleases God.

On the other hand, If we have no regard for God, we will be lost in his will for our lives per season. We will be gripped with confusion, fear, and anxiety. The fear of the Lord is indeed the beginning of wisdom (wisdom is the ability to discern what is edifying from what is harmful, and what is safe from what is dangerous) as stated in Scripture. However, the goal of wisdom is to align our hearts and values with that of God. We operate within the boundaries of God; love what He loves and hate what He hates. Just as toddlers' understanding of their parents goes beyond mere fear of their reactions when they do wrong, they begin to develop a relationship with them. They learn to recognize and understand what triggers their parents' reactions, leading them to refrain from those actions.

In our journey of faith, it is crucial to have a clear understanding of what God loves and hates. This knowledge allows us to align our lives with His will and purpose, and to discern between what is true and what is false. The Scriptures provide us with a comprehensive guidebook for navigating the complexities of good and evil. As we immerse ourselves in the study and meditation of God's Word, we gain insight into His character, His values, and His desires for our lives. The Bible serves as a reliable source of truth, revealing the nature of God and His standards for righteousness. Through its pages, we encounter stories, teachings, and principles that illuminate the distinction between good and evil. By studying the scripture, we develop a discerning spirit that enables us to recognize and reject falsehood. We become equipped with the knowledge and wisdom to identify deceptive ideologies, false teachings, and sinful practices. The Word of God becomes a lamp to our feet and a light to our path, guiding us away from the pitfalls of evil and leading us toward a life of righteousness. The Scriptures also reveal the heart of God, His love for humanity, and His desire for reconciliation and redemption. As we deepen our understanding of His love, we are compelled to align our lives with His desires and to love what He loves. We learn to hate evil not out of a place of judgment or self-righteousness, but out of a genuine desire to please God and reflect His character in our actions and attitudes. ***Proverbs 16:6*** states, ***"Through the fear of the Lord, evil is avoided."***

During my childhood, I had a memorable conversation with my father that has stayed with me. I must have been around the same age as JB. We were watching a movie that depicted drug use, and I remember my father turned to me and said, "If I ever catch you doing drugs, I am going to kill you." I interpreted his words literally and started crying uncontrollably. When my mom came home and saw me in tears, she looked at me and warned me sternly. I grew up thinking my parents were crazy and irrational. When I joined the military and smoked my first cigarette, I half-expected my Dad and Mom to come from behind and kill me! Now, I have observed that JB is not like me; he watches to see what gets his brothers and sisters in trouble and he does the opposite of that. He learns from other people's experiences about what is good and bad.

Unfortunately, many of us come to the knowledge of Good and Evil through our experiences. For instance, as kids, curiosity led us to stick the kitchen fork into the socket and earn a slap from mommy. That slap was what cautioned us from repeating the mistake. But as we grew older, we knew that sticking a fork to a socket could cause our death and refrained from doing so because we now have an understanding that that act is harmful. As Christians, many of us wait to learn from our experiences. We are determined to do our own thing until we experience the consequences. When we begin to reap the harvest of actions, instead of praying for God to deliver us from ourselves, we begin to attack the devil. However, that is the way of fools.

The remedy for a foolish heart is the wisdom and knowledge of God. Wisdom and knowledge come when we understand the reason behind God's disapproval of the things he hates. As a baby and untransformed Christian, we whine and refuse to hate what he hates. But, once we begin to fear God, we spend much time studying the word of God; we begin to understand why he hates what he hates, and loves what he loves and aligns accordingly.

The fear of God is birthed and nurtured in our hearts when we intentionally develop a relationship with God. Here is how you can cultivate an intimate relationship with God:

1. **Love God with all your hearts, souls, and might:** Give your whole being to loving God with passionate and genuine love. Let your affections, thoughts, and actions be directed toward Him, recognizing His supreme importance in your life.
2. **Yield yourself fully to God as your Lord and Master:** Surrender your will and desires to God, acknowledging Him as the ultimate authority over your life. Allow Him to guide and direct your path, trusting in His wisdom and perfect plan.

3. **Exalt Him far above anyone or anything else in your life:** Place God in the highest position of honor and reverence in your heart. Let nothing and no one take His place or diminish His significance in your life.

4. **Desire to know God deeply:** Cultivate a sincere thirst for a deeper knowledge and understanding of God. Seek to develop a personal and intimate relationship with Him, longing to know Him more intimately with each passing day.

5. **Consistently feast on the Word of God:** Regularly engage with the Scriptures, meditating on their teachings, and allowing them to shape your thoughts, attitudes, and actions. Let the Word of God be your guide and a source of wisdom and strength.

6. **Always be open with God and ask Him to convict you of any sins in your heart:** Maintain an attitude of openness and vulnerability before God. Humbly ask Him to reveal any areas of your life that are not

aligned with His will, seeking His forgiveness and guidance for repentance.

7. **Be in constant fellowship with God:** Cultivate a continuous and intimate relationship with God through prayer, worship, and communion. Seek His presence throughout your day, inviting Him to be an active and constant participant in your life.

By embracing these principles, you can deepen your love for God, grow in your understanding of His ways, and experience a vibrant and meaningful relationship with Him.

Love is the fundamental bedrock upon which all functional and thriving relationships are established. Similarly, our relationship with God is no exception. In our case, we are simply saying to God, "I accept the love you've shown me by sacrificing your only Son for my redemption and reconciliation with you." Loving God goes beyond mere emotional sentiment; it entails deliberate commitment and the prioritization of God above all else. It involves making a resolute decision in our hearts to live in a manner that is pleasing to Him and dedicating ourselves to serving His

Kingdom. By doing so, we open ourselves to deeper levels of intimacy with God. One key way to foster this intimacy is through constant fellowship with God. Just as relationships grow through regular interaction and communication, our connection with God flourishes when we engage in ongoing dialogue and companionship with Him. This entails spending time in prayer, studying His Word, and seeking His guidance and presence in our daily lives.

As we devote ourselves to this continuous fellowship, we not only strengthen our relationship with God but also unlock deeper levels of understanding, trust, and intimacy. Through our intentional devotion and unwavering commitment to Him, we deepen our love for God and experience the profound joy of walking in harmony with His will. In essence, love is the catalyst that fuels our relationship with God, and by actively pursuing this love and maintaining constant fellowship, we can cultivate a profoundly intimate connection with our Creator.

Can a relationship thrive in silence? The answer is yes! However, when it comes to our relationship with God, silence can lead to a sense of emptiness and doubt. When we neglect to engage in regular communion with God through prayer and studying the Bible, a void is created within our hearts. This void can impact our confidence in God and leave us uncertain about seeking His assistance. Just like in a scenario where a close friend suddenly becomes unreachable, doubts may arise about their willingness to help if we were to reach out to them. Similarly, when we lack consistent communication with God, our confidence in Him wanes, and fear takes advantage of this void, leading to doubt and uncertainty settling in. Maintaining regular and ongoing communication with God is crucial for nurturing a vibrant and steadfast relationship with Him.

Through prayer, we express our thoughts, concerns, and gratitude to God, while studying the Bible allows us to deepen our understanding of His character and His will for our lives. This constant connection and engagement with God's Word builds our faith, strengthens our confidence, and provides us with the assurance that He is always there for us. In this context, the fear of God refers not to a sense of dread but rather to a deep reverence and awe for His greatness, wisdom, and love. It is through this fear of God that we gain wisdom, understanding, and guidance for navigating life with confidence and boldness.

In conclusion, neglecting regular communication and communion with God can create a void within our hearts, leading to doubt and uncertainty. By embracing a consistent and intimate relationship with Him, we cultivate a deep reverence and fear of God, which serve as a foundation for wisdom and empower us to face life with confidence and boldness.

CHAPTER THREE

The Problem With Tomorrow

"Do not boast about tomorrow, for you do not know what a day may bring."

(Proverbs 27:1)

Tomorrow poses a challenge as we struggle with our attitude toward it. The truth is, tomorrow never truly arrives; it's always just another today. When we ponder about tomorrow, some of us become overly self-assured and arrogant, believing that our current circumstances will ensure success in the future. They boast about what they will achieve, being overconfident in their abilities. On the other hand, some excessively worry about tomorrow, allowing fear and anxiety to prevent them from taking action and having faith. To begin, let's explore the first perspective more deeply.

The peril of arrogance lies in our misguided belief that we can accurately predict tomorrow's course. We may be lured into thinking we possess a crystal ball that foresees the future just because our carefully laid-out plans appear to unfold smoothly. While feeling pleased and fulfilled when things align as intended is expected, we must not anchor our confidence in a promising future solely on these achievements. Placing our trust solely in our ego and capabilities, rooted in past triumphs and present victories, can be dangerous.

We are choosing to lean on our understanding instead of trusting God completely (Proverbs 3:5). We overestimate our capabilities and underestimate the plans of God for us.

It's like building a house on shifting sands. This is what it means to boast about tomorrow. Boasting about tomorrow is an act of arrogance and pride that often leads us to disregard placing God as our top priority. Many of us may claim to be fully committed to God until it comes to trusting Him with our future. We want to be in control and dictate how our lives unfold, often treating God as a secondary figure, brought along for appearance's sake, while we take the lead. This is a common struggle that many believers face. We may find it easier to trust God in certain areas of our lives, such as our daily needs or specific challenges we encounter. However, we sometimes falter when entrusting our future to His care and guidance. We believe that we know what is best for ourselves and may become consumed by our ambitions, dreams, and plans, thinking we have the ultimate say in shaping our future. We may only turn to God when it is convenient or encounter challenges we cannot handle alone.

While making plans and approaching them confidently is essential, we must also recognize that our lives are ultimately guided by a higher power, God. Rather than putting all our confidence in our dreams and ambitions, we should humbly seek a deep and intimate relationship with God. By prioritizing this connection, we gain insight into His plans and lay a strong foundation for our lives. This means aligning our desires with His and surrendering our plans to His perfect will. Through prayer, studying His Word, and being open to the guidance of the Holy Spirit, we can discern His path and walk confidently in it. This perspective helps us avoid relying solely on our understanding and pursuing self-centered ambitions. Instead, we find fulfillment in pursuing God and His purpose for our lives.

Let's explore the other side of the spectrum, where some Christians struggle with fear and anxiety arising from difficult circumstances they face. These negative emotions can prevent them from fully experiencing the realization of God's promises in their lives. As we discussed earlier, fear and anxiety are powerful forces that can significantly impact our faith, hindering us from embracing the fullness of what God has in store for us. As Christians, we are called to trust

God's faithfulness, love, and ability to fulfill His promises. Nevertheless, when fear and anxiety grip us, they can distort our perspective and lead us to doubt God's goodness and provision.

These Christians, are clouded by the challenges and negative realities of today; their hope and faith are in shambles, making it difficult for them to see beyond the present circumstances. Their present circumstances weigh heavily on their hearts, and they find it challenging to find the strength and courage to move beyond their current situation. As this state of helplessness lingers, they realize that much time has elapsed without noticeable progress. It feels as if they are trapped in a cycle of setbacks, unable to break free and make meaningful strides forward. These individuals are plagued by self-doubt and negative thoughts, questioning whether anything good can come from their learning disabilities. They believe they are not intelligent enough to pursue the speaking career God has called them to. Their constant illness leaves them wondering if they will ever have the strength to fulfill God's vision and purpose for their lives.

Amid the economic downturn, recession, and layoffs, they find it difficult to see a way forward. They refuse to realize that God can use their weaknesses to demonstrate His strength and fulfill His purposes.

The main problem some of us trapped in this mindset face is that we believe we can only confidently pursue God's purposes for our lives once our flaws and imperfections have vanished. We eagerly anticipate the day when all our blemishes will fade away, thinking that it is only then that we can step forward with confidence. It leads to a constant state of waiting and delay that is not God-sponsored or evidence of faith. Unfortunately, many of us misuse the precious gift of "today" that God has graciously bestowed upon us. Instead of fully embracing and making the most of the present moment, we often fall into the trap of placing our faith and hopes solely in tomorrow.

This mindset leads us to procrastinate on taking necessary actions today, as we believe that tomorrow will be the ideal time to accomplish our tasks and pursue our goals. The problem with tomorrow is that it never comes. By constantly deferring necessary actions and responsibilities to the future, we hinder our progress and miss out on valuable opportunities that the present holds. Placing our faith solely on tomorrow is a form of self-deception. It gives us a false sense of security and perpetuates a cycle of delay and unfulfilled potential. We may convince ourselves that we will be more prepared, motivated, or capable of taking action in the future. However, we take no action, living a life filled with regrets and empty aspirations.

There is a story about a small diner owner who wanted to boost his business. To attract customers, he placed a large sign in the window advertising "Free Lunch Tomorrow." As people noticed the sign, they took note of it and eagerly returned the following day, only to find that the sign remained in the window without fulfilling any free lunch offer. This is a person who has great plans for his business. He has diligently done market research and possesses a deep understanding of his product and the demand for it. He's done everything that should set him up for substantial profits. However, one thing obstructs him from enjoying his labor: he decides to give the free lunch tomorrow. How often have we fallen into this pattern? We devise beautiful plans and ideas for what we want to do, but they remain stagnant and unrealized. Nobody has more ideas than a person in jail: They often have a surplus of great ideas and plans for what they will do once released. They dream of a future filled with positive changes and outstanding accomplishments. For some of us, this is the exact story of our lives; we come up with brilliant ideas and make promises to ourselves about what we will do in the future. Maybe God has given you big dreams and plans for the future, but you find yourself stuck in inaction. You may intend to go to school next year or commit your life fully to God next week, but in the present moment, you feel unprepared and unable to take that leap.

This tendency to delay and make excuses hinders our progress and growth. It prevents us from living out the potential and purpose that God has placed within us. We may find ourselves waiting for the "perfect" time, waiting until we feel ready, or waiting for circumstances to align in a certain way before we take action. But here's the truth:

There will never be a perfect time. We cannot boast that tomorrow will come when we suddenly feel prepared and ready to fulfill life's purpose. We may only feel partially ready or have everything perfectly lined up. It is essential to recognize the issue James addresses regarding our plans for our lives versus God's plans for us. Often, we operate in God's plans the same way we operate in our plans, which often results in inaction or procrastination. James describes this approach as foolish because it places all our focus and confidence in a tomorrow that is not guaranteed. ***Proverbs 27:1*** says, ***"Do not boast about tomorrow, for you do not know what a day may bring."*** The issue with fixating on tomorrow is that it often leads to the constant postponement of God's plan for our lives. Instead of living in alignment with God's will, we keep pushing back our commitment to His purpose. James reminds us of the importance of seeking God's guidance in everything we do. We should consult the Holy Spirit to ensure our actions align with God's will. This may seem daunting and stressful, but James also emphasizes limited time. He compares life to a fleeting mist and reminds us of the urgency to live according to God's purpose and not to delay or waste time. We are not permitted to defer what can be done today to tomorrow.

Many of us find ourselves constantly caught up in the planning cycle for tomorrow, diligently outlining the habits we intend to cultivate, the books we aspire to read, and many other plans. This tendency arises due to various factors and influences in our lives. Procrastination stands as the primary factor among these influences.

I often find myself falling into bad habits, realizing that I only reach for my Bible when I need a word from God or study when exams are approaching. I have noticed that I don't spend enough quality time with God, and this week, I experienced feelings of anger, frustration, and even depression because I have been pouring into others without taking the time to nourish myself. In one of Joyce Meyer's teachings, she made a powerful comparison between tithes and offerings. Just as we give God a portion of our income and experience His blessings on the remaining 90%, the same principle applies to our time. If we feel like we don't have enough time for God, she suggests giving Him even more time. Nothing given to God is ever lost, and His blessings multiply unexpectedly. However, before I can fully seek after the things of God, there is an enemy within me called Procrastination. It hinders my progress and pulls me away from pursuing God wholeheartedly. What's the deal with procrastination? How does it impact our tomorrow? Let's dig into the definition and biblical insight.

In the concluding verse of James chapter 4, James addresses a frustrating sentiment, as it spoke directly to my struggles. He states that knowing what is right to do but failing to take action is considered a sin. Notably, James does not explicitly mention it as a sin against God; rather, it implies that we are essentially sinning against ourselves, hindering our potential and purpose. When we refuse to do what we should do, we rob ourselves of the life that God has designed for us, missing out on the blessings and fulfillment that come from living in alignment with His will. It is a self-sabotage that keeps us from stepping into the abundant life God has promised us. Procrastination can be defined in different ways. For instance, the American Heritage Dictionary defines it as "To put off doing something, especially out of habitual carelessness or laziness." Similarly, the Merriam-Webster Collegiate Dictionary describes it as "To put off intentionally the doing of something that should be done." The Oxford English Dictionary provides a definition of procrastination that captures the essence of its irrational and detrimental nature. It defines procrastination as a postponement, "often with the sense of deferring though indecision, when early action would have been preferable," or as "defer[ing] action, especially without good reason." It's delaying or postponing tasks or actions, even when we know we need to get them done. It's like constantly hitting the snooze button on our responsibilities, choosing to procrastinate instead of taking action on time.

You can relate to the experience of procrastinating, believing that you will do something later, only to find that time has slipped away and you have failed to fulfill the promises you made to the Lord. It often begins with the intention to do something later, whether in prayer, studying the Bible, serving others, or pursuing God's calling for our lives.

However, as time passes, we may find ourselves caught up in distractions, busyness, or a sense of complacency. This tendency to delay or put off our commitments is what we refer to as the sin of procrastination. It is a subtle sin that Satan often exploits, luring us into complacency and preventing us from taking action when we should. One of the ways Satan exploits procrastination is by planting seeds of doubt and fear in our minds. He whispers lies that make us question our abilities, doubt God's faithfulness, or convince us that there is always a better time in the future to act. By succumbing to procrastination, we become trapped in a cycle of inaction and missed opportunities.

The longer we delay, the harder it becomes to break free from procrastination. We may find ourselves making excuses, giving very cogent yet flimsy reasons for our inaction, and ultimately settling for a life that falls short of God's best for us. As I reflect on my life, I can't help but ponder on the missed opportunities that have come my way. It's not due to financial constraints, although money can slow our dreams. Looking back, I could have always found a way to save money if I had prioritized those opportunities. Moreover, despite my race and socioeconomic status, I can't say I had no opportunities because God always favored me with open doors. The missed opportunities that I lament today are solely my own doing. If only I had acted more promptly, made decisions, and remained steadfast despite the challenges. Unfortunately, procrastination has robbed me of these valuable opportunities.

Many of us desire greater joy, peace, love, financial stability, and good health. However, only a few follow through when taking effective and positive action to bring about these changes. We are entrapped in wishful thinking and lack the commitment to pursue what we desire actively. We hesitate to make difficult choices, step out of our comfort zones, and take responsibility for our goals. Think about this: Are you still in the same situation today as you were a year or several years ago, despite expressing the intention to change your circumstances? Have you made unfulfilled promises to yourself, others, or the Lord long ago? If so, it's essential to recognize that you are in a state of procrastination. You have allowed time to slip by without taking the necessary steps toward achieving your goals or addressing the areas of your life that require transformation. Procrastination can abort your progress and keep you stuck in inertia.

The Bible warns us sternly against procrastination. ***Proverbs 13:4 (ESV)*** warns us, ***"The soul of the sluggard craves and gets nothing, while the diligent soul is richly supplied."*** Cravings evoke strong emotions. It depicts an intense longing that ripples through our entire being. When we experience cravings, it's as if our whole being becomes consumed by the object of our longing. It occupies our thoughts, stirs our emotions, and evokes a powerful sense of wanting. One incredible moment in the life of a newly married man is witnessing how incredibly intense and compelling his pregnant wife's craving is, incredibly late in the night when all she wants is pickles and ice cream. Her desire for particular foods or experiences can become so intense that they dominate conversations, thoughts, and daily activities. He may join her on late-night trips to the store, searching for specific ingredients or unusual food combinations to satisfy her cravings. That's how powerful cravings are, they consume us. Yet the Bible says the sluggish has these cravings, intense longings, and desires, yet gets nothing. The lofty dreams, the daily fantasies, the journals, and the written goals all fizzle into nothing because they find their way into the heart of a sluggard who dreams and wakes up to eat the bread of idleness. Cravings never pull a man out of hunger. Cravings do nothing to improve the health and finances of anybody. Its diligence– the choice to damn procrastination and everything that paralyzes your ability to work toward your dreams -satisfies your cravings.

Procrastination leads to poverty. Let's look at ***Proverbs*** *24:30-34*

"I passed by the field of a sluggard, by the vineyard of a man lacking sense, and behold, it was all overgrown with thorns; the ground was covered with nettles, and its stone wall was broken down. Then I saw and considered it; I looked and received instruction. A little sleep, a little slumber, a little folding of the hands to rest, and poverty will come upon you like a robber and want like an armed man."

Here is a man blessed with an opportunity to grow something beautiful. He was given a field like a blank canvas waiting to be filled with life. He could have planted anything he wanted: wheat, corn, vegetables, flowers. He could have created something beautiful that would bring others joy. But the man did nothing. He let the field go to waste. He lets the weeds grow tall, and the ground becomes hard. He let his opportunity slip away. Like the ungrateful servant in the parable of the talents, who was given one talent but buried it in the ground instead of using it to make a profit, the man in the field was lazy and irresponsible. He refused to take care of his field, and instead of soaring with the wings of the opportunity he was given, he chose to slide through life.

Many of us are like this. We are allowed to grow a ministry, start a business, or plant a church, and we are excited about the possibilities. We pray, we dream, and we make plans. But then, something happens. We get busy. We get distracted. We start to make excuses. And before we know it, the opportunity has passed us by, and we are left feeling unfulfilled and frustrated. I am a victim of this too. I have had many opportunities to be fruitful in my ministry, but I have not always been faithful to follow through.

I have made excuses, procrastinated, and let my fears get in the way. But I am learning. I am learning that God expects me to be fruitful, and I am determined to do better. God has committed great things to us. He has made us heirs and co-laborers in His vineyard. He has allowed us to make a difference in the world. And He expects us to be fruitful. But, just a little sleep, a little slumber, a little listening to the opinion of others, a little trying to dodge the lessons during our waiting period, a little...a little...a little this or that and we fail to succeed in our land we've been given to cultivate. The alarm clock rings at 2:30 AM, its shrill sound piercing the silence of the night. You roll over and try to ignore it, but it's useless. You know that you're supposed to be praying and communing with God now, but the sleep that hangs heavily on your eyelids is too tempting. You close your eyes and tell yourself that you'll pray tomorrow night. The next night, you do the same thing. And the night after that. And the night after that. Two months go by, and you still haven't honored your date with the Holy Spirit. It's no wonder the weeds have overgrown your crops, choking out the flowers and fruits you worked so hard to grow.

Procrastination robs us of so much. It is a thief that steals our time, energy, and potential. It robs us of the opportunities to shine as lights in the world. When we procrastinate, we let weeds grow in our lives rather than the flowers. Instead of blossoming into a beautiful boulevard of flowery attractive gardens with lush and green trees, blooming flowers, and the sweet scent of nature, peace, and tranquility, we become like an abandoned wild forest. God has a blueprint for our lives even before we were formed in our mother's womb. But what happens when we procrastinate? When we procrastinate, we let the weeds grow in our lives. We are choosing to let our potential go unfulfilled. We are choosing to not become all that God has destined us to be. We make it look like God has not equipped us with talents. We make it seem like we are not battle axes meant to be sharpened. But if we refuse to be sharpened by God through the experiences He calls us to, the batches He wants us to bear, and the marks that will serve as our identity in Christ, we become like cold woods that cannot bring a spark to the plan of God. I have been asked to preach months in advance, but I often procrastinate and don't start working on the message until the night before. This leaves me feeling anxious and worried. I could have delivered the message with power if I had started earlier, but my procrastination greatly affected the quality of my delivery.

Our generation has a hard time sacrificing and enduring pain. We work hard to feed our addictions but find it challenging to work for the things that matter. Instead of actively seeking opportunities and filling out applications, we wait for handouts. We quickly accept the wrong job that takes us away from what was getting us sober. We say we'll go to a meeting tomorrow, but tomorrow never comes. We find it hard to break free from addictions because of procrastination. Procrastination in recovery is deadly because it is born out of pride. Pride keeps us from humbling ourselves and asking for help. It keeps us from going to meetings or calling our mentors. It keeps us from falling on our knees and asking God for deliverance. Millions of people are less than they could be because they procrastinate. They wait for tomorrow, but tomorrow never comes. The stress of procrastination can crush us, and our health can decline. We may even turn to drugs to give us energy, and we may find ourselves fighting depression. Procrastination is a habit that can be difficult to break, but it is not impossible. If we are willing to face our fears and take action, we can overcome procrastination and live our lives to the fullest.

Why We Procrastinate

According to the Bible, there are five underlying reasons why we tend to procrastinate.

1. Indecision

Indecision is a common problem that can significantly impact our lives. It can lead us to postpone important decisions, such as buying a car, choosing a college, or getting married. It can also lead us to make poor decisions simply because we are unable to make up our minds. The Bible warns us about the dangers of indecision. In ***James 1:8,*** we are told that ***"a double-minded man is unstable in all he does."*** This means that when we are indecisive, we are not sure what we want, and this can lead us to make rash decisions or avoid making decisions altogether. Indecision can hurt our lives in many ways. It can lead to stress, anxiety, and frustration. It can also prevent us from achieving our goals and living our best lives.

If you are struggling with indecision, there are a few things you can do to overcome it. First, it is essential to identify the root of your indecision. Are you afraid of making the wrong decision? Are you worried about what others will think? Once you understand the root of your indecision, you can start to address it. Don't forget to run everything under the lens of God's word and the Holy Spirit's nudging. Take it to the Lord in prayer, he can help you make a solid decision. ***James 1:5-8 (ESV)*** states, ***"If any of you lacks wisdom, let him ask God, who gives generously to all without reproach, and it will be given him. But let him ask in faith, with no***

doubting, for the one who doubts is like a wave of the sea driven and tossed by the wind. That person must not suppose he will receive anything from the Lord; he is double-minded, unstable in all his ways." This passage highlights the necessity of seeking wisdom from God when facing indecision. We are encouraged to approach Him in faith without doubting His ability to provide guidance. Doubt and double-mindedness lead to instability and hinder our ability to receive answers from the Lord.

2. Perfectionism

Ecclesiastes 11:4 offers a powerful reminder regarding perfectionism: ***"He who observes the wind will not sow, and he who regards the clouds will not reap."*** If we wait for perfect conditions or circumstances, we will never take action or experience fruitful outcomes. Perfectionism is a common problem that can prevent us from taking action. We may be afraid of making mistakes, so we wait until everything is perfect. However, this can lead to procrastination and inaction. Perfectionism can harm our lives in many ways. It can lead to stress, anxiety, and frustration. It can also prevent us from achieving our goals and living our best lives. We may never start or give up on a project halfway through because it is imperfect. Perfectionism makes us compare ourselves to others and be afraid to take risks.

When pursuing God's will, we must understand that perfection does not lie within our control or our perception of what is perfect. Instead, Scripture assures us that every good and perfect thing comes from God Himself. Therefore, it is essential to let go of the notion of perfection and instead trust in God's timing and provision. *2 Corinthians 12:9 (ESV)* says, ***"But he said to me, 'My grace is sufficient for you, for my power is made perfect in weakness."*** God's grace is enough to sustain us in our weaknesses and imperfections. We should rely on His strength rather than our efforts.

3. Fear

Fear is a common emotion that can prevent us from taking action. We may be afraid of failure, rejection, or humiliation. However, if we let fear control us, it can lead to procrastination. The Bible warns us about the dangers of fear. In Proverbs 29:25, we are told that "the fear of man is a trap." Suppose you have been putting off essential actions like visiting the dentist, undergoing necessary surgery, seeking marriage counseling, or sharing your faith at work. You should ask yourself, "What am I terrified of?" Fear often paralyzes us and prevents us from taking necessary steps toward our well-being or fulfilling our God-given purposes. However, the Bible encourages us to trust the Lord, finding safety and security in Him rather than succumbing to the grip of fear.

The Bible tells us that ***"there is no fear in love, but perfect love casts out fear" (1 John 4:18).*** When we experience the depth of God's love, our fears diminish as we trust His goodness and grace. However, when we experience the love of God, our fears begin to melt away. We realize that we are loved unconditionally and that nothing can separate us from the love of God. This knowledge gives us the courage to face our fears and live confidently. There are many ways to experience the love of God. We can experience it through prayer, reading the Bible, spending time in nature, and our relationships with others. When we open our hearts to God's love, we see the world through His eyes and realize that we are loved and valued beyond measure.

4. Anger

Procrastination is often seen as a sign of laziness or lack of motivation. However, it can also be a form of passive resistance. When we procrastinate, we say, "I don't want to do this." This can be a way of expressing our anger or frustration with a situation or with someone else. The Bible warns us about the dangers of anger. In ***Proverbs 18:9***, we are told that ***"a lazy person is as bad as someone destructive."*** There are many reasons why we might procrastinate. We might be afraid of failure, we might be feeling overwhelmed, or we might simply not want to do the task. However, when procrastination is motivated by anger, it can be a way of getting back at someone we don't like. For example, imagine your boss asking you to do a task you don't want to do. You might procrastinate by saying, "I don't like you telling me what to do." This is a form of passive resistance, and it can express our anger without actually saying anything.

5. Laziness

Proverbs 13:4 in the Living Bible highlights the contrasting outcomes between lazy individuals and those who are diligent: ***"Lazy people want much but get little, while the diligent are prospering."*** In America, the word "easy" is very appealing. We tend to gravitate toward tasks or endeavors that require minimal effort. Conversely, when faced with challenges or demanding situations, we are inclined to shy away from them. Consider, for instance, the unlikelihood of a best-selling book titled "Ten Difficult Steps to Change Your Life" or "Fifteen Challenging Ways to Get in Shape." We naturally lean toward ease and convenience while displaying reluctance toward arduous endeavors. However, the wisdom found in Proverbs reminds us that pursuing an easy path often leads to limited results. Laziness hinders productivity and impedes progress, causing individuals to desire much but achieve little. Conversely, those who embrace diligence and a strong work ethic find themselves prospering and experiencing tremendous success in various areas of life.

The best attitude we should have about tomorrow is to learn from the life of Jesus. In ***John 9:4,*** Jesus said, ***"I must work the works of Him who sent Me while it is day; the night is coming when no one can work."*** Jesus had an attitude of urgency and confidence. He never worried about completing the work of His Father, nor did He compromise or succumb to laziness and procrastination. We should also have this mind in us. Like Jesus, we should focus on working today and not put it off until tomorrow. We should stop procrastinating on what we can do now. Tomorrow, the following Monday, next year, when we have more money, or when we lose weight—who knows when our "night" will come and we will no longer be able to work as expected?

CHAPTER FOUR

Watch Your Mouth

"Whoever restrains his words has knowledge, and he who has a cool spirit is a man of understanding. Even a fool who keeps silent is considered wise; when he closes his lips, he is deemed intelligent." (Proverbs 17:27-28 ESV)

How we communicate reflects our character, just as God's word reflects His character. Our words possess a profound and often underestimated power. According to the teachings of the Bible, there are no idle words; each word we speak has the potential to propel us forward or pull us backward in life.

It's like driving a manual transmission car: when in neutral, the car will roll toward the incline of the ground beneath it. Similarly, if our words lean toward negativity, they will influence our path accordingly.

Our words are not mere empty sounds or symbols but actual forces that carry weight and shape our lives. They hold the capacity to create and transform. This power of words is evident in our daily lives as they can build or break relationships, inspire or discourage people, and promote positive change or spread hatred. The impact of our words is far-reaching, more significant than we often realize.

Words are the building blocks of our worlds. If ***"the universe was created by the word of God so that what is seen was not made out of things that are visible" Hebrews 11:3 (ESV)***, why do you think words are not building materials? Now that we are here, let's talk about God's creative power. To create means to bring something into existence or to make something new that did not exist. To create is to breathe life into something that was once an idea. It is giving birth to something else. Creating also has to do with bringing order out of chaos and creating beauty out of ashes. What best fits this beautiful definition of what it means to create? It is the zenith of God's creation. After uttering, ***"Let us make in our image and likeness,"*** God spoke man into existence. He used the most unlikely building materials—earth, soil, and dirt. Out of dirt came a beautiful creation capable of housing God's spirit. You can pick up a mirror and see your face. It's fantastic that we came from words. Just as God spoke the universe, our words can create something new. When we create, we tap into a creative force that mirrors the divine act of bringing something new into being. Words help us to bring things to reality. A mere glimpse at the Book of Genesis showed us how the beautiful and luscious earth we live in was void and formless. Just a chaotic and empty mass of water. Can you try to paint the picture of the earth then: Unattractive and devoid of potential? With a litany of spoken "***let there be,***" God took this formless and void Earth and transformed it into a beautiful and bountiful world. He brought order to the chaos and light to the darkness. He created the sky and the sea, the land and the plants, the animals and the humans.

As creative as words are, they are also destructive. Words can build up or tear down. They can create relationships and destroy them. How many of us have started a day feeling enthusiastic and full of life, only to have our mood dampened by the terrible news about a loved one or a demeaning comment? The Tower of Babel was a project that was going well. Everyone worked together toward a common goal: to reach the heavens and communicate with God more personally. As they built the tower, brick by brick, they spoke the same language and had the same vision. God saw that this project was already completed because the people spoke the same language and had the same goal. He destroyed their ambition and thwarted their plans by confusing their languages. The people still spoke the exact words but could no longer understand each other. This destroyed their ambition and the project they had all agreed upon so passionately. By now, we have established that the power of words extends beyond their surface meaning.

Words possess a spiritual dimension, and depending on the content and intent behind them, they can attract either positive or negative spiritual influences. The Holy Spirit will back up our words if we speak truth, love, and peace. He will help us to see our dreams come true and to live a life of joy and abundance. Conversely, when our words are filled with negativity, deceit, or malicious intent, they can become vehicles for destructive influences. Like wings carrying dark forces, these words can sow seeds of discord, pain, and chaos. They can damage relationships, harm reputations, and create turmoil.

If words are spirits, could it be that we have spoken words concerning ourselves that are already working death within us? Have we carelessly uttered things responsible for our ill health and failing hearts? Jesus said in ***John 6:63b (NKJV), "...the words I speak to you are spirit, and they are life."*** He constantly speaks life to us. We know we have life if what we constantly say to ourselves and our situations align with what Jesus has told us. If our words do not align with what God has said about us, trust the Devil, he will stuff words in your hearts and lips that will bring you more chaos. Let's learn from Job in the Bible. This is a faithful, committed individual who, in our time, would have been a worship leader, cell unit leader, or even a great evangelical Apostle. The devil poorly afflicted Job, losing everything he had except for his wife. Despite his terrible suffering, his beloved wife, who was supposed to help him remain strong and relentless in his faith in God, advised him to curse God and die. This was not some recommendation from an enemy or a stranger but from his wife. While the centurion in Luke 8:5-13 confidently told God to say the words and his son would be healed, Job's wife advised him to say the words and die. Thankfully, he paid no attention to his wife's terrible advice.

Proverbs 18:21 (ESV) states, ***"Death and life are in the power of the tongue, and those who love it will eat its fruits."*** God, who created life through His words, has bestowed upon us the ability to shape reality with our speech. But sometimes, we use our words to hurt others. We say mean things to our friends and family and even mean things to ourselves. We must be careful about what we say because our words have power. The enemy knows this, and he uses our words against us. He wants to divide us and make us fight with each other. But we can use our words to build each other up. We can say kind things to each other and encourage each other. We can use our words to make the world a better place.

Have you ever received kind words from someone but found yourself questioning the sincerity behind their expressions? On the other hand, have any of your closest friends or loved ones uttered harsh words toward you, yet you quickly dismissed them because you know their hearts are consistently filled with kindness? The former scenario was God's dilemma in Isaiah 29:13. To an outsider, the Israelites may have seemed like passionate and devout people. They would have seen them worshiping God with great zeal and enthusiasm. However, God was deeply disgusted by their insincere worship and lip service because they were only going through the motions, and their words were not a true reflection of their heart. The connection between words and our heart conditions becomes evident in this context. Words carry significant power when they come from the depths of our hearts. Even in the context of salvation, the Bible teaches that we must first believe in our hearts and then confess with our mouths that Jesus is Lord to be saved. Belief precedes confession, as what we speak is an overflow of what dwells within our hearts. Our confession will be empty and meaningless if we do not believe Jesus is Lord. It is from the abundance of our hearts that our mouths speak (Mathew 12:34). The connection between our hearts and our words is a recurring theme throughout the Bible and holds significant importance in our lives. It reveals the intrinsic link between our inner beliefs, emotions, and the language we use. The scripture tells us that our words are not mere expressions but reflections of the condition of our hearts. In ***Luke 6:45***, Jesus states, ***"The good person out of the good treasure of his heart produces good, and the evil person out of his evil treasure produces evil, for out of the abundance of the heart his mouth speaks."*** This teaches us that our words indicate what is stored within us. If our hearts are full of good things, our words will be good too. But if our hearts are full of bad things, our words will be bad too. For example, if we have a heart full of love, we will naturally say loving things to others. But if we have a heart full of anger, we naturally say angry things to others.

Since words are borne from the heart, what do we do to get the well of our hearts filled with living waters that produce life when we speak? Many of us speak words of truth concerning our situations, hoping for a positive change. However, we often find that these words don't bring the desired change because deep down in our hearts, we question the reality of those words. For instance, we may say we are strong when we feel weak, but instead of improving, we worsen because our words lack genuine conviction. When we don't experience immediate relief, we tend to give up on affirming those words.

This is a problem of lack of faith. And this is caused by not hearing and internalizing the word of God. As stated in ***Romans 10:17, "Faith comes from hearing, and hearing through the word of Christ."*** When we neglect to immerse ourselves in God's word, we open ourselves to hear other things and our faith dwindles. We must guard our hearts at all times to ensure that spiritually ill and life-draining words are not being filtered into our souls and spirits. These words never leave us without triggering or even executing in full measure what they were intended for. This is why Proverbs 2:23 (NIV) says, "Above all else, guard your heart, for everything you do flows from it."

How Do You Guard Your Heart?

1. Watch who you allow to speak over your life.

Do you know about Jabez in the Bible? Quick! Let's head on to ***1st Chronicles 4:9-10 (ESV)*** and learn more about the story of this young man.

Jabez was more honorable than his brothers; and his mother called his name Jabez, saying, "Because I bore him in pain." Jabez called upon the God of Israel, saying, "Oh that you would bless me and enlarge my border, and that your hand might be with me, and that you would keep me from harm so that it might not bring me pain!" And God granted what he asked.

This is the story of a child whose mother, perhaps desiring a son but facing the challenges of pregnancy, consciously decided not only to speak negatively about her innocent baby but to pronounce words that would shape his entire life. A name is often the initial piece of information people learn about us. Just imagine the trauma of enduring pain while carrying the burden of a name that seemingly destined you for a lifetime of suffering. However, Jabez refused to let his mother's words dictate the course of his life. The people in our lives are constantly speaking over us. They may say things meant to build us up, or they may say things meant to tear us down. Just like Jabez, we may have no control over their words. Yes, it is traumatizing to hear demeaning statements from people, especially your loved ones, but it is irresponsible to wallow in the realms of their destructive words. It can be tempting to succumb to the destructive words of others because doing so relieves us of personal responsibility. It is easy to ride on the wings of their hurtful words and blame them for destroying your life. Resist that temptation and choose to fight for a new life like Jabez.

You may not control what others say, but you can selectively choose which words to embrace and which to let go of, like a bulletproof vest deflecting harmful ammunition. Don't let their words take root and grow; nip them in the bud. If you are fortunate enough to identify a particular relative or friend who consistently speaks negatively about or verbally abuses you, confront and counter those words through prayer. Cutting those conversations short is essential if your friends are consistently negative and demeaning. Likewise, if gossip dominates their discussions, it's best to do the same. ***Proverbs 8:7-8 (MSG) states: "Fools are undone by their big mouths; their souls are crushed by their words. Listening to gossip is like eating cheap candy; do you want junk like that in your belly?"*** Surround yourself with positive individuals who uplift and challenge you to grow. Advocate for yourself and refuse to allow anyone to speak hurtful words or curses over you. When expressing your thoughts, do so with love and kindness. There's no need to be rude or self-righteous, but be clear and assertive. Most importantly, never let anyone silence you or suppress your voice. Let them know that you do not appreciate demeaning conversations.

2. Watch what you allow into your gateways

It is essential to be mindful of the things we allow to pass through our gateways, just as it is essential to be mindful of the people we allow to speak into our lives. Our eyes and ears are gateways to our spirit, influencing our thoughts, emotions, and overall well-being. *Matthew 6:22-23 (NIV)* says, ***"The eye is the body's lamp. If your eyes are healthy, your whole body will be full of light. But if your eyes are unhealthy, your whole body will be full of darkness. If the light within you is darkness, how great is that darkness?"*** I know people who watch a lot of crime dramas become skeptical and scared. Their eyes became unhealthy; these shows are often filled with violence, death, and deception. They can give people a warped view of the world and make them believe everyone is out to get them. I say this all the time, you must guard your gateways. What are you seeing?

What are you listening to? Many Americans have vowed against marriage because of the traumatizing news of domestic violence and divorce we pay attention to. You should also be careful with your words as your mouth serves as another gateway.

Paying attention and acting accordingly is essential if you sense a little twinge or a fleeting hesitation in your spirit. If you ignore the prompting of the Holy Spirit, He will be quiet, which is a scary place to be. Most of us ignore this little nudge of the Holy Spirit, spend hours unending scrolling through social media, ingesting all those toxins, and expect to live an everyday spiritual life. Put on spiritual blockers and pay less attention to the content that does not illuminate you.

Let's talk about music. To grasp how powerful music is, it's pertinent to revisit the story of David and Saul. Saul, the first king of Israel, was tormented by an evil spirit from God. He experienced fits of rage and troubled emotions. To keep him sane and calm, Saul's servants suggested that he bring David to play the harp for him. The Bible says that ***"when David***

played the harp, Saul was relieved of his suffering and became well, and the evil spirit left him" (1 Samuel 16:23 NIV). Music kept Saul sane! A lot of us are running amok because of the kind of songs we let into our spirits. For example, listening to artists like 2Pac may provoke you to fight even while at work. At the same time, artists like Gates may have a desire for intimate connections. It's not to say that we should only listen to Christian music, but it's essential to guard our ears and be attuned to the guidance of the Holy Spirit in our music choices. The Bible recommends you fill yourself with psalms, hymns, and spiritual songs, singing and making melody to the Lord with your heart (Ephesians 5:19 ESV).

How To Speak

When we speak, air from our lungs goes through our throats and reaches the voice box. Inside the voice box are two folds of tissue called vocal cords. As the air passes between these cords, they vibrate, creating sound. These are the intelligible or unintelligible words we hear. These words, in turn, shape our realities: abate wars, break relationships, please God, or destroy our lives. There is a way to speak as Christians who want to know God experientially.

When you have a challenging time dealing with your little boy, and parenting feels difficult, there's a way to speak that doesn't harm your child. Similarly, when we encounter fellow Christians who we believe have strayed from the right path, we should learn to communicate in a manner that doesn't break them down. We must be mindful that there are no idle words, and every word we speak will be accounted for. When we wake up and experience slight discomfort, we might say, "Oh, I'm getting sick." As we go about our day, we repeat these negative statements, such as "I feel horrible." Eventually, we may start feeling unwell and even express things like "I'm dying." This is the wrong way to speak. Instead, imagine if we chose to say, "Thank you, Lord, for another day of waking up." We acknowledge any bodily discomfort but focus on the positive aspect of still being able to move and function.

Sometimes, we find ourselves saying mean things about ourselves to gain sympathy. In desperate situations, we use our words to worsen our circumstances further. However, it's important to remember the power of our words and how they can impact our lives. *James 3:4-8 (NASB)* gives an analogy about the tongue's influence. ***"Look at the ships also, though they are so great and are driven by strong winds, are still directed by a tiny rudder wherever the inclination of the pilot desires. So also, the tongue is a small part of the body, and yet it boasts of great things. See how great a forest is set aflame by such a small fire! And the tongue is a fire, the very world of iniquity; the tongue is set among our members as that which defiles the entire body, and sets on fire the course of our life, and is set on fire by hell."*** Our words possess tremendous power. They can inflict minor wounds that fester into severe problems or bring about healing and restoration. The tongue is a fire, you can use it to refine or destroy. The choice is yours! I recommend speaking God's words. The Word of God is alive and powerful. It can destroy any adverse situation and build up healing and restoration for you. For example, you can speak healing scriptures over your body if you struggle with sickness. You can declare that the stripes of Jesus heal you and that your body is the temple of the Holy Spirit. You can speak prosperity scriptures over your finances if you are struggling financially. You can declare that you are blessed to be a blessing and that you have more than enough to meet your needs. The Word of God is powerful because it is the truth. When you speak the truth, you are aligning yourself with the power of God. You are calling forth the power of heaven to work in your life.

In addiction recovery, we use affirmations to help us stay on track. Addiction is a complex and challenging issue that can have a devastating impact on individuals, families, and communities. For those who are struggling with addiction, the road to recovery can be long and difficult. However, there are several effective tools and strategies that I use to help people overcome addiction and live healthy, fulfilling lives. One of these tools is the use of affirmations. Affirmations are positive statements that are repeated regularly. I use it to help people who are trying to break free from drugs, anxiety, and depression to change their negative thoughts and beliefs about themselves and their addiction. It instills feelings of confidence, hope, and optimistic thinking, and encourages them to adopt positive and beneficial actions. When leading these recovery classes, we use affirmations like "I am loved unconditionally by God", "I am strong and capable of overcoming my addictions", and "I have a sound mind". Affirmations are powerful because they reprogram your mind. Instead of focusing on hateful and draining thoughts that can crush you, your mind begins to learn how to think healthily and soundly. The best affirmations are repeating again and again what God says about you.

To know what God says about you, you need to read His words. However, simply reading it isn't enough; you must also believe it. And the way to foster belief is by consistently speaking God's truth daily. Faith comes by hearing. You must repetitively open your soul and spirit to the showers of God's truth and be immersed in it. Admittedly, it's not always easy to maintain this practice. There will be days when you won't feel like it, but interestingly, those are when you need it the most. During those challenging times, speaking God's truth becomes even more crucial. It's vital to fill yourself up with the word of God. It is the most outstanding blocker we have against the lies of Satan. Many of us wear sunscreen to reduce the effect of the sun's harmful rays on our skin. In like manner, we must put on the armor of God's words to fight off negative words that destroy our lives.

When I'm going through a tough time, I need a constant reminder of God's love, grace, or any specific need. I find a scripture that speaks to me and write it on my bathroom mirror. I see it every morning and night and read it repeatedly until it gets into my spirit. During my time in the military, I suffered an injury that required multiple surgeries. The pain that followed was not only physical but also emotionally draining. It took a toll on my mental well-being, causing me to slip into depression. As I struggled with the overbearing pains, I found myself repeatedly saying things like, "I will always be in pain," believing that this suffering would be a permanent part of my life. The pain was so severe that it made it difficult to focus on anything else. I would wake up in the morning feeling depressed and I would go to bed at night exhausted. I knew that I needed to take control of my thoughts and mindset. I realized that the negative self-talk I was engaging in was only making things worse. I began to affirm the comforting words of God to myself. I started by writing down a list of positive affirmations that I could repeat to myself whenever I felt down. These affirmations were words like, "I shall not die, but live." I also started reading the Bible and seeking out passages that reminded me about God's love and mercy. We all need these reminders, and I assure you that a simple Google search for "Scriptures about (your situation)" will yield hundreds of relevant verses. Additionally, you can consult the back of your Bible or utilize resources like YouVersion, where you can find scriptures addressing a wide range of topics. There is a scripture for everything. The Bible says that there is nothing new under the sun. This means that whatever you are going through today, someone in the Bible has gone through something similar. You can find comfort and encouragement in their stories and know you are not alone.

Revelations 12:11 (NLT) says, ***"And they have defeated him by the blood of the Lamb and their testimony. And they did not love their lives so much that they were afraid to die."*** The "him" mentioned here represents the devil, our common enemy. We have already defeated the devil by the blood of the Lamb and our testimony. Jesus defeated him already, **BY THE BLOOD.** And our testimony, the words of our mouth, will show others. How does God get any glory if you are silent about your struggles? When you tell your story, do you glorify the behavior of the good old days? Do you take credit for your healing? Do you give credit to a program or a person? When you tell your story upwards, directing their attention toward God? Proverbs are distinguished from other wise sayings because they consistently direct our focus upward. Proverbs encourage us to align our thoughts, words, and actions with God's wisdom and guidance. This perspective helps us live according to God's truth and bring glory to His name.

Years ago, my daughter came home from school upset. She was always dramatic, and if you knew her, you'd understand. However, this time it was different. She was genuinely sad because someone told her she had no friends. Instead of brushing it off, she held onto that hurtful comment. After comforting her, we took the opportunity to challenge the lies she had believed. We reminded her that she did indeed have friends, and she had many people who loved and cared for her deeply. The enemy would have dragged her to a dark place if she had continued to dwell on the lie. Our children are killing themselves, cutting, and overdosing because they can't tell the difference between the truth and lies. We must teach them how to recognize lies and speak the truth over themselves.

Before You Speak, Ask Yourself These Questions:

- Is what I am about to say relevant to the issue, or am I speaking from a past hurt?

- Will it cause division?

- Will the person I'm talking to receive it well? Not everyone is ready to hear wisdom.

- Should I pray before I speak?

- Does it need to be said, or am I simply stating the obvious?

- Will it make the person or yourself feel worse about something?

- Am I speaking out of emotion or fact? Remember, feelings aren't facts.

- Is it true?

- Am I gossiping?

- Will this be encouraged?

- Am I just agreeing to be nice?

In conclusion, the most crucial aspect of our communication is measuring our words against the truth in God's words.

Understanding our words' power, we must diligently align them with the principles of love, compassion, and wisdom as demonstrated by our Creator.

By constantly evaluating our speech against the standard of God's truth, we can ensure that our words become instruments of positivity and encouragement. Let us remember that our words have the potential to impact not only our lives but also the lives of those around us. Therefore, we should use them wisely and responsibly, mindful of their immense influence.

As we strive to reflect God's character through our words and actions, may we also cultivate a heart of humility, seeking forgiveness for any words that may have caused harm or pain. By choosing to speak truth, love, and kindness, we can contribute to a world where our words serve as a source of inspiration, healing, and hope.

CHAPTER FIVE

Why Am I So Mad

"A man who is hot-tempered will stir up strife, but he who is slow to anger, he will calm contention." (Proverbs 15:18 NASB)

Anger is an intense human emotion that everyone experiences from time to time, and it can arise in response to various triggers or frustrations. Joyce Meyer describes it as the most powerful, strongest, and dangerous of the three most harmful negative emotions. It surfaces when we feel threatened, frustrated, or when our desires are not met. Like other primary emotions such as joy, sadness, fear, and surprise, anger is a fundamental aspect of our psychological makeup. Anger signifies that something awful is stirred inside of us. It's a reaction to a perceived injustice done to us or others. While anger is a natural emotion, it's essential to learn how to manage it healthily.

The problem is not that you get angry but what you do because of your anger. The Bible says, ***"Be angry, and do not sin; do not let the sun go down on your wrath" (Ephesians 4:26).*** In God's design, anger is a legitimate emotion that is a part of being human. It can serve as a powerful catalyst for change, but we should not overlook its potential to cause havoc and harm if not properly managed.

It is okay to get angry, as long as we do not raise our hands at our spouses, throw things at our siblings, and utter despicable words at others. For some of us, anger becomes intertwined with our darker tendencies, making us act on our vices. Anger can simmer deep in our hearts, like a dormant volcano. When provoked, it can erupt unexpectedly, causing us to lash out, say hurtful things, and behave in ways that are out of character. We are often taken aback by our actions and surprised at the intensity of our reactions.

As the Bible instructs, managing anger without sinning can be like attempting to fall a tree with a razor. It is a painful struggle. You may be pierced and bruised by the sharp venom spilled at you, yet your heart still feels bitterly wronged. You may try to suppress your anger, but it hangs heavy in your chest, and you can only imagine feeling lighter if you could retaliate or inflict terror on the source of your anger. When anger flares up, it can be accompanied by a rush of adrenaline and an impulse to react harshly. It is such a powerful emotion that clouds our thinking and sense of judgment. In the heat of the moment, self-control may feel like an elusive goal, and we may find ourselves struggling to respond in a godly manner.

There must be a reason God instructs us to be angry yet not succumb to unspeakable actions. Throughout history, the consequences of unchecked anger have been evident, like in the tragic tale of Abel and Cain. These two brothers, both devoted to God and offering Him their first fruits, found themselves in a bitter rift that led to devastating consequences. The younger brother lost his life while the eldest brother was sentenced to a useless life. How tragic! Cain initially desired to worship God with his offering of fruits from his labor. However, when his offering was not accepted in the same manner as his brother Abel's sacrifice, anger began to take root within him. Instead of addressing his emotions healthily, he allowed his anger to fester and grow unchecked. Cain went from being a worshipper to a murderer.

Frequently, we come across heartbreaking news stories of wives who murder their husbands they once deeply loved, unable to bear the burden of their actions. Many of us start serving God in various capacities within the church with pure intentions, only to find ourselves inadvertently serving the devil's wicked schemes due to unresolved anger. Feelings of mistreatment by church leaders and members can transform the fire that once fueled our zeal and devotion into intense and persistent hatred. While we may sing praises to God with our lips, our hearts become clouded by anger, making it challenging to feel God's presence.

What gives rise to anger? What fabrics are woven together to create this unsightly blanket capable of shrouding even nations in turmoil, pain, and regret? What lies at the root of these devastating circumstances that leave even the most devout Christians in solemn regret? This force has the power to undermine leaders like Moses and drive nations into conflict. What precisely plants the seed of discord in a union that was once the envy of others, captivating their attention and causing even the devil to shudder in fear? What exactly is the root cause of anger?

There is no single culprit we can blame as the sole root cause of anger. Anger is a complex emotion that can arise from a myriad of factors and experiences. As human beings, our emotions are influenced by various internal and external factors, making it challenging to pinpoint a single source of anger. It can be triggered by personal frustrations, perceived injustices, unmet expectations, hurtful words or actions, and even past traumas. However, James gives us a clue to the root cause of anger. ***James 4:1-2 (NIV) "What causes fights and quarrels among you? Don't they come from your desires that battle within you? You desire but do not have, so you kill. You covet but you cannot get what you want, so you quarrel and fight. You do not have it because you do not ask God."***

James highlights the connection between jealousy and anger in the human heart. Jealousy can create a void within us, a hole in our hearts that becomes filled with anger. When we allow ourselves to be enticed by what others possess, often at the cost of appreciating our blessings, we start despising ourselves and magnifying our weaknesses. Instead of addressing these dangerous seeds, our hearts become consumed with rage and anger toward others and we begin to fight them.

When we study the Bible, we see that there are two distinct kinds of anger: righteous anger and unrighteous anger.

Righteous Anger

Righteous anger is motivated by a desire to do what is right and just. It is often accompanied by a sense of injustice or unfairness. It is a response to actions that are contrary to God's will and principles. Righteous anger is fueled by a divine fire that burns brightly within the hearts of those who hold fast to their faith. It is not a rage driven by petty grievances or personal vendettas; instead, it is the desire to pursue and defend what is holy and just. In the New Testament, we see instances where Jesus and some of the Apostles' hearts were ablaze with righteous anger, yet their passion was never tainted by bitterness and wrath.

When Jesus entered the temple in Jerusalem and found merchants and money changers conducting their business, He was filled with righteous anger. The temple was meant to be a holy place, a house of prayer, and a symbol of God's presence among His people. Yet, it had been turned into a bustling marketplace, where commercial interests overshadowed the spiritual purpose of the temple.

He saw this desecration of His Father's house, and His response was one of passionate zeal for the sanctity of the temple and the reverence due to God. He overturned the tables of the money changers, and He drove out those who were buying and selling, declaring, "My house shall be called a house of prayer, but you make it a den of robbers." This act was not motivated by personal gain, selfish desires, or pettiness. Instead, it was a manifestation of Jesus' deep love and devotion to His Heavenly Father and a reverence for the sacredness of the temple. He could not bear to witness God's dwelling place being profaned by commercial activities that distracted him from the true purpose of worship and prayer. Jesus' actions were not vengeful or destructive.

During the early days of Christianity, there was a significant debate among the followers of Jesus about whether Gentile (non-Jewish) converts should be required to follow Jewish customs and laws, particularly circumcision and dietary restrictions. Some Jewish Christians believed that these practices were essential for salvation, while others, like Paul, emphasized the concept of justification by faith in Jesus

Christ alone. At one point, Peter visited the Christian community in Antioch, which was a city with a mix of both Jewish and Gentile believers. When Peter arrived, he would eat with the Gentile Christians, disregarding the Jewish dietary laws. He believed in Paul's teaching of freedom in Christ for both Jews and Gentiles.

However, the situation changed when some Jewish Christians, who believed in strictly following Jewish customs, arrived in Antioch. In fear of their opinion and to avoid conflict, Peter started separating himself from the Gentile Christians and refused to eat with them. Paul saw this behavior as a contradiction to the gospel of Jesus Christ, which emphasized unity and equality among believers, regardless of their ethnic backgrounds. He was angry and rebuked Peter openly because his actions compromised justification by faith alone and instead suggested that Gentiles needed to adhere to Jewish customs to be fully accepted by Christ. Paul's anger was justified and not motivated by selfish gains.

Righteous anger is often a call to action, to search oneself and ensure we are still sticking to the faith that was handed over to us. it does not seek to harm but to heal, not to divide but to unite, not to tear down but to build up. It does not aim at sowing seeds of bitterness and resentment but rather gives way to forgiveness and grace. It is surely not driven by pleasures or personal gain; it can be a heavy burden. Can you imagine what people must have thought about Jesus? A savior who was saddled with the responsibility of drawing people to God driving them away from the presence of God. Righteous anger can be a burden, but because it burns with a fierce intensity, people like Paul could fight for the Gentiles to be included in the Gospel of Salvation.

Unrighteous Anger

In Jeremiah 17:9, God describes the heart of man as being desperately wicked. As descendants of Adam and Eve, we inherited a sinful nature, which inclines us toward selfishness and wickedness. This sinful nature affects our thoughts, desires, and actions, making it difficult for us to consistently choose what is right and good. Unrighteous anger is a common response to hurt or offense, and it stems from our fallen nature. When we feel wronged or hurt, our immediate reaction may be to retaliate or seek revenge, wanting the other person to experience the pain they caused us.

When someone hurts us, it ignites this restlessness and wrath within us, we may feel an overwhelming urge to strike back, adding fuel to the flames. Just like a fire spreads and consumes everything in its path, unrighteous anger seeks to destroy and hurt others in its wake. The hurt we experience acts as the spark that starts this fire of anger. The more we dwell on the pain and nurse our wounds, the stronger the fire grows. Instead of trying to extinguish the flames with wisdom and self-control, we allow it to rage out of control. Just as a wildfire can quickly get out of hand, unrighteous anger can spiral into destructive behavior, leading us to lash out verbally, hold grudges, or take actions we may later regret. This uncontrolled anger clouds our sense of better judgment and makes us blind to the consequences of our actions and the need to forgive and let go.

In Galatians 5:19-21, the Apostle Paul provides a list of works of the flesh, which includes unrighteous anger. Let's take a closer look at the relevant passage:

"Now the works of the flesh are evident: sexual immorality, impurity, sensuality, idolatry, sorcery, enmity, strife, jealousy, fits of anger, rivalries, dissensions, divisions, envy, drunkenness, orgies, and things like these. I warn you, as I warned you before, that those who do such things will not inherit the kingdom of God." (Galatians 5:19-21 ESV)

Within this list, "fits of anger" (also translated as “outbursts of wrath” or “unrighteous anger” in other versions) is mentioned as one of the works of the flesh. This refers to the kind of anger we've been discussing, which is uncontrolled, vengeful, and harmful to others. The reason Paul includes unrighteous anger in this list is to highlight the importance of self-control and living a life guided by the Holy Spirit. Throughout the New Testament, we see consistent teaching about the transformation that should occur in the lives of believers after they accept Christ as their Savior. Unrighteous anger is considered a work of the flesh and is inconsistent with the Spirit-led life that believers are called to live.

You know, it's fascinating how unrighteous anger can be like molten magma. When something or someone hurts us, that anger inside us can just bubble up like a fierce explosion. It's like we're about to blow our top! No one can stand us at that moment. We blurt out unspeakable words that can damage our relationships with friends and family and we say things we don't mean. Just like molten magma cools and turns into solid rock over time, unrighteous anger can also change its form. It might not be as obvious as when we're in the heat of the moment, but it can still be there, hidden away beneath the surface. The problem with this hidden anger is that it can be just as harmful. It's like a dormant volcano, waiting to erupt at any moment. It might not be out in the open, but it's still eating away at us from the inside. It can make us bitter, resentful, and even hateful if we don't deal with it properly.

Ephesians 4:26-27 says, ***"Be angry and do not sin; do not let the sun go down on your anger, and give no opportunity to***

the devil." This is talking about time. Time can be both a blessing and a curse when it comes to unrighteous anger. While time can allow wounds to heal and emotions to settle, it can also solidify our anger. The Bible warns us to desist from giving our object of anger a breeding ground. A lot of us cultivate anger, we fan the flames and keep waiting for the moment to let it go burst. When you let the sun go down on your anger, you create barriers around your hearts. the walls of resentment and bitterness grow stronger and taller, the only thing it can accommodate is the devil. At this point, It's very difficult for the word of God to guide your emotions.

Silent anger can be devastating; the longer we hold on to it, the more destructive it becomes. One of the reasons we resort to silent anger is fear - fear of confrontation, fear of being vulnerable, or fear of being hurt again. We might carry wounds from the past, be it from childhood experiences, traumatic events, or moments when we faced injustice. These unhealed wounds can fester over time, leading to silent frustration and unresolved anger. The struggle with silent frustration is that we feel unable to express it openly.

We might fear being judged, misunderstood, or rejected if we share our deepest pains and traumas. As a result, we stuff these emotions inside, and they can remain hidden for years, buried deep within our hearts.

But let's consider the contrast by imagining if God had held on to His anger when Adam sinned against Him in the Garden of Eden. Instead of offering a means of reconciliation, imagine if God had chosen to remain silent in His anger and distance Himself from humanity forever. The consequences of such a decision would have been devastating for us and even for God Himself. We would have been left in a state of eternal separation from our Creator, with no hope, forgiveness, or redemption. Our relationship with God would have been irreparably broken, and we would have been forever condemned by our sins.

God was able to find means for our reconciliation because of the boundless love that resides in His heart. Despite being rejected and disobeyed by humanity, God's love prompted Him to reveal His immense love for the world by offering His Son, Jesus, for the salvation of all. Conversely, when our already wicked and selfish hearts are burdened with unprocessed hurt, it's like a raging war within us. The pain, bitterness, and unresolved emotions wage a battle that affects not only our inner peace but also our outward expressions. As the Bible says, ***"Out of the abundance of the heart, the mouth speaks."***

If we refuse to renew our minds as Romans 12:2 commands us to, instead, conform to the hurt in our hearts, we heap coals on an already blazing heart. When our hearts are filled with unprocessed hurt, the words that scream within us are often words of hatred and strife. Although we might try to maintain a bright countenance on the surface, underneath, we carry a heavy burden of silent wars. These wars rob us of inner peace, leaving us tired and worn out, affecting our emotional well-being, relationships, and overall outlook on life.

Anger is a secondary emotion because it stems from deeper underlying feelings or experiences. When we experience anger, it is like a fruit that has grown from the seeds of other emotions or circumstances. There are three main sources from which anger can arise:

1. **Powerlessness:** When we experience situations or circumstances that make us feel powerless, anger can be a natural response.

2. **Fear:** Fear is another potent source of anger. When we encounter situations that trigger fear or anxiety, anger can be an instinctive reaction.

3. **Inferiority Complex:** When we feel like we're not as good or important as others, it can make us angry. This anger comes from a strong desire to protect our self-worth and dignity.

Anger is like a fruit that grows from a deeper root, and that root is often fear, particularly the fear of what others think about us. Even though anger might be the visible emotion on the surface, deep down, it comes from a heart that feels scared, insecure, unsafe, and lacking trust. This heart is seeking something from other people that only God can truly provide.

Anger usually manifests itself in three distinct ways;

1. **Explosive and Blowing Up:** This form of anger is characterized by sudden outbursts and emotional explosions. When someone experiences explosive anger, they might lose control of their emotions, raising their voice, shouting, or even becoming physically aggressive. It's like a volcano erupting, releasing pent-up emotions with great intensity. In this state, the person might feel a sense of power over others, attempting to assert themselves through forceful behavior.

2. **Stewing, Brewing, or Silent Indignation:** This type of anger is the opposite of explosive anger. Instead of venting emotions outwardly, people with this form of anger keep their feelings inside, like a pot simmering on the stove. They might appear calm on the outside, but inside, they are filled with frustration and resentment. This can create an atmosphere of tension, and people may notice them walking on eggshells, afraid of setting off their hidden anger. People may

say things like, "Is everything okay?" because they sense something is wrong with them.

3. **Irritability, Exasperation, or Embitterment:** This form of anger is characterized by being easily annoyed, frustrated, or bitter. The person might snap at others over small things or become impatient and short-tempered. It's like a constant simmering of annoyance just below the surface, ready to boil over at any moment. While this anger might not be as visibly explosive as the first type, it can still harm relationships and create a negative atmosphere.

It's important to understand that silent anger, which is the second form, can be just as offensive to God as explosive anger. While the expression might be different, the underlying emotions and attitudes are still rooted in anger. The Bible cautions against giving in to anger and advises us to be slow to anger (James 1:19-20) and to avoid sinning in our anger (Ephesians 4:26-27).

The Angst of Anger

Regardless of how anger manifests, the angst of anger can have significant effects on us. One of the areas that it affects deeply is our spiritual health. Anger has the potential to gnaw at our spiritual well-being, slowly eroding the peace, joy, and connection with God.

1. Cycle of Strife and Sin

Proverbs 29:22 says "A man of wrath stirs up strife, and one given to anger causes many transgressions." A person who is hot-tempered starts fights and creates chaos almost everywhere they find themselves. For some people, anger can become an addiction. It makes them feel a burst of energy and pleasure, similar to how some people feel when they take drugs. They're easily ignited at the slightest provocation. Like a raging inferno, their anger consumes them and makes them blind to reason and restraint. They may hurl hurtful words, be reckless with their actions, and even become willing to cross lines they would otherwise never dare to approach. Anger becomes a gateway to all kinds of sins; It can cause us to make harsh judgments, hold grudges, and become aggressive. In extreme cases, it can even lead to violence and death.

The story of the baseball game and the ensuing brawl shows how anger can start a destructive cycle, much like the story of Cain from the Bible. In the spring of 1894, the Baltimore Orioles arrived in Boston for a regular baseball game. However, the events that unfolded that day were far from ordinary. During the game, a fight broke out between John McGraw of the Orioles and the Boston third baseman. Soon, all the players from both teams were involved in the brawl. The conflict escalated, spreading to the grandstands and among the fans. Shockingly, someone set fire to the stands, and the entire ballpark was engulfed in flames. The fire didn't stop there, as it spread and damaged 107 other buildings in Boston. Just as a small fight between two players quickly escalated into a huge fire that spread to many buildings, anger can also escalate and spread. In the case of Cain, his anger towards his brother Abel led him to commit a terrible act of murder. This had consequences not only for Cain but also for his descendants.

2. Broken Relationships

In the hustle and bustle of our daily lives, we often put on a facade, displaying a cool and collected demeanor at work or in public. We greet our colleagues with a warm smile, yet at home, our patience wears thin and we greet our loved ones with outbursts of anger. We might find ourselves snapping at our family members over trivial matters, raising our voices in irritation, or reacting with anger to the slightest inconvenience.

The ones who look up to us for care and comfort now face the brunt of our emotional storm. Uncontrolled anger can have a big and lasting effect on our relationships. When we frequently express anger or have a tendency to react explosively, it creates an atmosphere of tension and fear within our circle of family and close friends. As a result, they may find themselves walking on eggshells around us, trying their best to avoid triggering our anger. Our loved ones may choose to keep their thoughts and feelings to themselves, avoiding conflict. This can make it difficult to have open and honest conversations, which makes it difficult for them to bond with us. Our children may not tell us about a problem they are having at school, for fear of being punished. A partner may not express their concerns about the relationship, for fear of starting an argument. We may find our friends not being able to share their true feelings about a situation, for fear of hurting our feelings.

The constant fear of provoking our anger can lead to emotional distancing. Our loved ones might withdraw emotionally, keeping their thoughts and feelings guarded to avoid conflict. This emotional distance can strain the intimacy and closeness we once shared.

3. Being Influenced By The Spirit Of Anger

In Romans 6:16, Paul explains that we become slaves to whatever spirit we choose to obey. If we consistently allow the spirit of anger to govern our lives and actions, over time, it will gain control over us, shaping the way we relate to others and impacting our emotional well-being. When we allow anger to control us, we are essentially letting our emotions dictate our actions and interactions with others. In doing so, we impose our power over others, subjecting them to the negative consequences of our uncontrolled anger.

When we allow anger to rule over us, it can become a tool for the devil to sabotage the blessings God intended for us. God desires to bless us with meaningful and fulfilling relationships that serve as channels for His blessings in our lives. However, when anger consumes us, it can sever those very relationships that were meant to be sources of support, love, and encouragement. Our anger can drive a wedge between us and our family members, friends, and colleagues, causing rifts that may be difficult to mend. Anger can strip us of the very things that God intended for us to enjoy and cherish. It can rob us of the blessings that come from healthy relationships, stable jobs, and the possessions we hold dear. It creates a void in our hearts and lives, leaving us empty and disconnected.

On the other hand, if we exercise self-control over our anger, we allow God's power to work within us through the Holy Spirit. Controlling our anger doesn't mean denying its existence; instead, it involves managing it healthily and constructively. When we submit to God's guidance and invite the Holy Spirit to lead us, we receive the grace to control our anger and be delivered from the influence of the spirit of anger.

Dealing With Anger

Ephesians 4:27 warns us not to give the devil a foothold in our lives. A foothold is like a secure spot where the devil can gain a hold and start to exert influence. It's similar to letting him put his foot in the door, giving him an opening to enter and cause havoc. When we allow unresolved anger and unprocessed pain to linger in our hearts, it allows the devil to work his way into our lives. If we hold onto grudges, nurse bitterness, or refuse to forgive, we create a foothold for the devil to exploit. He takes advantage of these negative emotions to build a stronghold in our minds.

A stronghold is like a fortified castle or fortress, where the devil sets up his base of operations. It becomes a place from which he launches his attacks on our thoughts, emotions, and actions. The longer we allow anger and negative emotions to fester, the stronger this stronghold becomes, and the more control the devil gains over our lives. But the good news is that we have the power to resist the devil's advances. The Bible tells us to resist him, and he will flee from us (James 4:7). This means that we can actively fight against the devil's influence in our lives by relying on the strength of our faith and trust in God. By surrendering our anger to God and choosing forgiveness and love, we weaken the devil's foothold and dismantle his stronghold in our hearts.

However, it's essential to understand that resisting the devil is an ongoing process that demands courage and faith. He won't give up easily, and he'll keep trying to find new ways to gain a foothold. That's why we must remain vigilant and committed to allowing God's love to be shed abundantly in our hearts.

In addition to this, it's important to give yourself to prayer and ask God to help you deal with anger by putting these principles into action:

1. **Admit that you are angry:** The first step to dealing with anger is to admit that you are angry. Sometimes, we might try to deny or suppress our anger, but being honest with ourselves is important. Recognizing and admitting our feelings of anger opens the door to healing and closes the door to bitterness and pent-up emotions.

2. **Identify the root cause of your anger:** Understanding the root cause of our anger is essential. It might be triggered by past experiences or unmet expectations. Anger is often a secondary emotion, meaning it is triggered by another emotion. For example, you might feel angry when you are feeling hurt, scared, or frustrated. Identifying the source of our anger enables us to address it more effectively.

3. **Ask yourself, "Is this the best way to express my anger?":** When you are feeling angry, it is important to take a step back and ask yourself if this is the best way to express your anger. Will yelling, screaming, or name-calling solve the problem? Or will it only make

things worse? Often, we may respond to anger with reactive and impulsive behavior. Instead, we can consider healthier alternatives, like calmly communicating our feelings or taking a break to cool down before addressing the issue.

4. **Spend time praying for the difficulty that you have in handling this emotion:** When you are struggling to deal with your anger, it is important to pray for help. God understands our emotions and desires to help us navigate through them with wisdom and grace. Romans 8:26 assures us that the Spirit of God comes to our aid when we face weaknesses, including the difficulty of handling certain emotions like anger. We can bring our weaknesses before Him in prayer, He helps us gain insight into the root causes of our anger and enables us to break free from the cycle of destructive anger. When we feel overwhelmed by anger, God through the help of the Holy Spirit gives us peace and helps us to respond more constructively.

5. **Focus on forgiving others:** Holding onto grudges and unforgiveness only fuels our anger and keeps us trapped in negativity. By choosing to forgive, we release the power that anger has over us and free ourselves from the burden of bitterness.

6. **Try to understand why the other person did what they did**. This doesn't mean you have to agree with them or condone their behavior, but it does mean trying to see things from their point of view. Forgiveness is not something that happens overnight. It is a choice that you make over and over again. Decide that you are going to forgive the other person, even if you don't feel like it. Once you have decided to forgive, it is important to let go of the anger. This doesn't mean forgetting what happened, but it does mean not letting it control your life. Lastly, Praying for the other person can help you to release your anger and bitterness. It can also help you to develop compassion and understanding for them.

CHAPTER SIX

The Joy Of Surrender

Trust in the Lord with all your heart, and do not lean on your own understanding. In all your ways acknowledge him, and he will make straight your paths. (Proverbs 3:5-6 ESV)

God created us out of his divine love and purpose and embedded in us a delicate feature – the power of choice. He was not some tyrant when he conceived and executed the creation of man. After He had intricately designed us after His image and likeness to have dominion over everything,

His greatest desire was for us to choose Him. As a parent, you may take your adorable babies out for some treats. As they receive candies from you, their faces light up with joy and excitement. Now, playfully ask them to give back what you just gave them. Some of them might pout cutely and giggle, reluctantly handing back the goodies. Others, with tiny hands tightly clutching the treats, might reluctantly return them to you. God extends His goodness and blessings to us. He lavishes us with His life and grace, hoping that we will joyfully respond to His kindness. He patiently waits for us to willingly give back our lives to Him.

Surrendering to God means committing our ways entirely to the LORD, placing our trust and confidence in Him, and allowing Him to take control and fulfill His promises in our lives. It entails willingly yielding ourselves, our wills, desires, and plans, to the loving care of our God. It is a conscious decision to let go of self-reliance and self-rule, and instead, entrust our lives entirely into God's hands. In surrender, we acknowledge God's sovereignty and supreme wisdom, recognizing that His plans for us are far greater than anything we could orchestrate on our own.

Surrendering to God involves casting all our cares, worries, and anxieties upon Him. It means recognizing our limitations and human frailty and acknowledging that God is the ultimate source of strength and provision. When we surrender, we choose to release the burden of trying to control every aspect of our lives and instead place our trust in God.

Surrendering is not a passive act; it is a conscious decision to seek God's guidance and direction in all our decisions. It means involving Him in every aspect of our lives, consulting Him before making choices, and aligning our will with His divine plan. ***1st Peter 5:6-7 (NIV)*** says ***"Humble yourselves, therefore, under God's mighty hand…"*** Surrendering to God requires humility because it means acknowledging that, despite our education, intelligence, and accomplishments, we may never fully understand the intricacies of our creation or realize the blueprint God has for our lives. It is an admission that we are not self-sufficient and that we need

God to steer our journey. In a society that often celebrates independence and self-made success, it takes humility for the average American to admit that they do not have all the answers. Many people often fall into the trap of thinking they can handle everything on their own. They believe that they can control their destiny and achieve their goals through their efforts. This may not look harmful or destructive, but as Christians, living outside the will of God sets us up for failure because God knows us intimately, even before we were conceived. He knows our strengths, weaknesses, and the purpose for which He created us. What's better than just taking orders from God and handing over the reins of our lives to Him?

We may find surrendering our wills and plans to God very challenging, especially when we are faced with uncertainty and societal expectations. In Mark 10:28, After following Jesus for a while, Peter left his trade and fishing business behind. He had seen Jesus perform multiple miracles, but he still wondered what was in it for him to follow Jesus. Life is a journey with ever-changing phases. In one season, our focus may be on pursuing education, and we might not worry about having kids. However, as time goes on, especially after getting married, thoughts of starting a family can consume our minds. Comparisons with others add to the pressure. We see our peers achieving success and abundance, while it seems like the devil delights in hindering our progress. It's as if our temples are permeated with stress, and we wonder why our efforts aren't bearing fruit as we hoped.

When we are weighed down by the overwhelming burden of daily life, many of us desperately yearn for an escape, a way to release our sorrows and feel light, even if only for a fleeting moment. We crave rest so intensely that we seek it through various outlets, even if it means resorting to substances that promise a temporary feel-good sensation. Sometimes, we may look at a peaceful river and feel drawn to its calmness. We imagine lying there, letting its soothing waters take away all our problems. We daydream about floating away, escaping from life's difficulties, and entering a world of bliss where nothing troubles us. As you take a leisurely evening walk through the city parks and busy markets, you can't help but notice the heavy atmosphere of sadness. Many people seem worn out, depressed, and on the brink of giving up. They hold on to a fragile thread, fearing it might snap and end their lives.

Surrendering to Jesus is not just a clichéd response but the only way to find hope and survival in this dying world. In the dark and chilly Garden of Gethsemane, Jesus himself faced a make-or-break moment – a gut-wrenching decision whether to submit to God's plan or abandon the very mission that could redeem mankind. The weight of impending death bore down on Him, and the battle inside His heart was fierce. He desperately wished for the "cup of death" to be taken away from him. However, amid his pains and trepidation, He mustered the courage to surrender to the will of His Father. Despite the pain, humiliation, and excruciating death on the cross that stood before Jesus, He still surrendered to God's will. It was a surrender unlike any other, one that brought about a cosmic shift. Jesus forever altered the destiny of humanity. His surrender to God paved the way for those who sat in darkness, consumed by the weight of their past to see the light. Now, just like Jesus, we have the chance to experience the joy of surrender. It might not always be easy; the world might tempt us to take a different path, one that promises fleeting pleasures and false securities. But the truth remains – the only true rest, the only genuine peace, lies in wholeheartedly yielding ourselves to God.

Surrendering Our Emotions

As Christians, submitting our emotions to God can be one of the most challenging aspects of our faith journey. We may declare with our lips, but deep inside, we still struggle with worries, anger, and fear that seem to grip our hearts tightly. Many of us carry emotional baggage from the past – painful experiences, traumas, and disappointments that have left scars on our hearts. We let these wounds linger and affect our present relationships and well-being. God wants us to surrender the twists and turns of our emotions to him; From the exhilarating highs of joy and laughter to the heartbreaking lows of sadness and frustration. He wants to be in control of them because our emotions reside in the realm of the flesh and if left unchecked can lead us astray.

In the Bible, there is a tragic story, where unchecked emotions revealed a chain of events that led to terrible consequences. Amnon, David's son, found himself captivated by the beauty of his step-sister, a pure and virtuous young woman. His heart became so entangled in his desire that he wore a sad and haggard countenance. Instead of taking his infatuation with God, Amnon chose to confide in the wrong person. There's no harm in confiding in people but you must be certain that your confidant is surrendered to God, one who can view the situation through the lens of God's word, pray for you, and provide a perspective that aligns with God's standards. Unfortunately for Amnon, the advice he received from Jonadab was poisonous; instead of encouraging him to seek God's help in handling his emotions, he devised a deceitful plan to fulfill Amnon's desires. The consequences of not surrendering his emotions to God were quite glaring. From a pure and harmless infatuation that God could have handled to intense hatred and death.

Amid our warring emotions, we may not be in the right frame of mind to make sound judgments, but thankfully, we have an advocate we can always trust. David, a man who truly understood the importance of being open and transparent before God, offered this valuable advice in ***Psalm 62:8 (ESV), "Trust in him at all times, O people; pour out your heart before him; God is a refuge for us."*** God is our safe haven and we can be vulnerable before him. We don't have to hide our struggles or put on a facade of strength. God invites us to come as we are, with our joys and burdens, lust and love, hatred and bitterness, confident that He receives us with open arms and transforms our hearts. Just as David enjoyed the mercies of God whenever he surrendered to God, we can live knowing that our raging emotions are taken care of.

Surrendering The Future

The future is filled with uncertainties and it is only natural for us to be filled with anxiety when contemplating what lies ahead. We may often find ourselves asking questions like, "What will my future be like?" or "Will I achieve my dreams and aspirations?" My mom carried a heavy burden of worry about our future, and her concerns were not unfounded. My oldest sibling had been caught up in the dangerous street life for years. Living in a community filled with drugs and violence, she feared that my younger sister and I might also be lured into that path. Our present challenges may validate the fears we have concerning the future but what if we just choose to surrender to God and trust Him? Many of us struggle to surrender our future to God because we tend to trivialize the past miracles He has already performed in our lives. He miraculously helped us graduate from college, yet we find ourselves anxious and worried about finding a job. We easily forget the ways God has provided for us in the past and allow our fears to overshadow His faithfulness. When we look back at all the times God has intervened on our behalf, it should give us the confidence that He will continue to be with us and guide us in the future.

The Israelites had firsthand experience with God's miraculous power. He rescued them from the oppressive rule of Pharaoh, performed numerous plagues against their enemies, and led them out of Egypt with great signs and wonders. You would think that such a people, having witnessed God's mighty hand at work, would fully trust Him to lead them to the promised land. However, when the journey to the promised land began, their trust in God quickly wavered. A journey that should have taken 40 days ended up stretching over 400 years. Why? Because they allowed fear, frustration, and impatience to consume them. Instead of relying on God and surrendering to His plans, they focused on their immediate needs – hunger, thirst, and discomfort. They began to murmur, complain, and curse God because they lost sight of God's faithfulness. ***"They did not remember his power or the day when he redeemed them from the foe"*** *(Psalm 78:42 ESV).*

In the same way, we, too, struggle to surrender our future to God when we let our fears and worries take center stage. God's love and faithfulness are constant, and He wants us to rely on Him for our future. Let's see ***Matthew 6:28-33 (ESV)*** to understand why God wants us to surrender our future to Him. ***"And why are you anxious about clothing? Consider the lilies of the field, how they grow: they neither toil nor spin yet I tell you, even Solomon in all his glory was not arrayed like one of these. But if God so clothes the grass of the field, which today is alive and tomorrow is thrown into the oven, will he not much more clothe you, O you of little faith? Therefore do not be anxious, saying, 'What shall we eat?' or 'What shall we drink?' or 'What shall we wear?' For the Gentiles seek after all these things, and your heavenly Father knows that you need them all. But seek first the kingdom of God and his righteousness, and all these things will be added to you."***

If God takes care of even the smallest details in nature, like the flowers of the field, these flowers do not toil or spin to clothe themselves, yet they are adorned with beauty beyond compare. How much more you, the zenith of His creation? Instead of being consumed by worries about food, clothing, and the uncertainties of the future, focus on God's kingdom and His purposes for you. When you prioritize your relationship with God and align your heart with His will, you can confidently entrust your future into His hands.

Surrendering our future does not mean we sit idly by, expecting God to do everything for us. Instead, it involves active participation in seeking God's will through prayer, seeking His guidance through His Word, and making decisions with a surrendered heart. It means submitting our applications and resumes for that job and resting your heart in God's favor. It means buying the baby clothes in faith knowing that God opens the womb of the barren.

How to Surrender to God

When we feel the slightest physical pain, we often turn to painkillers without hesitation, trusting in their healing properties. When hunger strikes, we rely on food to satisfy and nourish us. Trust is at the core of these actions, as we believe in the efficacy of these remedies. Similarly, when it comes to surrendering our lives, emotions, and future to God, trust plays a pivotal role. If we lack trust in God, surrendering becomes a daunting task. Abraham surrendered to the call of God and left his family and familiar surroundings because he trusted God. Similarly, Noah's trust in God helped him stay focused and determined on the assignment God committed to him even in the face of ridicule and mockery from the people of his time.

Now that we understand that trust serves as the foundation for surrendering to God, let's explore practical steps to build that trust in Him. These steps will help us develop the confidence and faith needed to surrender our lives, emotions, and future entirely to God.

1. Meditate on God's word: Psalm 63:6-8 (ESV), "When I remember you upon my bed and meditate on you in the watches of the night; for you have been my help, and in the shadow of your wings I will sing for joy. My soul clings to you; your right hand

upholds me." Meditation is not just reading the Bible passively. It is hearing what God is saying to you, reflecting on His word, contemplating His promises, and focusing your thoughts on His character and ways. When we intentionally meditate on God's word, we open our hearts to him, tune out distractions and worldly concerns, and fill our souls and spirits with the sure words of His prophecy. Jesus said the words He speaks to us are life (John 6:63), if we are not immersing ourselves in them, we may get worked up, consumed in fear, and die of worry.

2. Surrender Daily: When you have armed yourself with the truth of the word of God, as you go through the challenges and realities of life, you will be tested, and that's why intentional surrender is vital. Each day, take the time to surrender your life, desires, and worries to God. Let go of control and trust in Him. By doing so, you nurture the faith that meditating on God's word has instilled in you. Just like watering a

plant to help it grow, daily surrender helps your relationship with God flourish.

The joy of surrender is experiencing true rest amidst life's chaos. It is being enveloped in a peace that surpasses our understanding, attained when we release our burdens and fears and place our trust in God's perfect timing. It is being anxious for nothing and placing our trust in God. Even in times of global turmoil, when nations may go to war and economies may face recession, we can have peace, knowing that God's promises are steadfast and true. He is faithful, and what He has promised will always come to pass.

CHAPTER SEVEN

The Power of Forgiveness

"Love prospers when a fault is forgiven, but dwelling on it separates close friends." (Proverbs 17:9 NLT)

When people talk about forgiveness, its meaning can be complex because people understand it differently. Forgiveness is a multi-layered concept; many people from different backgrounds have diverse opinions and thoughts about it. This concept is often at the heart of deep and traumatizing human experiences, and it evokes many emotions that influence individual perspectives of forgiveness. Some see it as a posture of strength, while others perceive it as a sign of weakness and foolishness, as they are concerned it might make them vulnerable to their offender. Amid these diverse perspectives, what does the Bible say about forgiveness?

When we set out to understand faith and the act of surrender, we will find valuable insights into the lives of patriarchs like Abraham and Job. These men show us how to trust and submit to God's will without hesitation, teaching us valuable lessons for our spiritual growth. However, if we seek to delve into the heart of a man who passionately pursued God and sought to be aligned with His desires, the focal point of our study would undoubtedly be David. In the scriptures, we see how much David longed after God's heart. He expressed this through his psalms, prayers, and continuous dedication to God. Similarly, for an exceptional case of personal transformation and remarkable accomplishments in God's kingdom, we can examine the life of Paul. When Paul had a life-changing encounter with

Christ on the road to Damascus, he went from persecuting Christians to becoming one of the most influential apostles and evangelists in history.

This goes without saying that to grasp the significance and essence of forgiveness, our attention should turn to our heavenly Father. He is the ultimate example of forgiveness for us to explore. In the annals of human history, the greatest offense ever committed was mankind's rebellion against God. Despite the countless times we have hurt Him through our disobedience and rejection; God still shows us mercy and forgiveness.

Forgiveness is the decision taken to liberate ourselves from the burden of resentment and pain. When we forgive, we consciously choose to release ourselves from the grip of hurt caused by others or even from the wounds we inflict upon ourselves. It means extending pardon and understanding to those who have wronged us, or to ourselves when we acknowledge our imperfections and mistakes.

After Adam's act of rebellion against God, he listened to the deceitful voice of the serpent instead of heeding God's commandment and a massive rift ensued between him and God. Adam and Eve went from reveling in the intimate presence of God during the cool evenings – enjoying a harmonious and loving relationship – to withdrawing from God's presence. While it was Adam and Eve who had disobeyed God's command, it was God Himself who had been deeply hurt by their rebellion. God had every reason to unleash His anger and forever turn away from us. He could have lamented the very act of creating mankind, regretting the gift of free will that allowed us to choose between good and evil. He could have halted the entire creation plan. However, because of God's very nature of love, instead of turning away from us in anger, He decided to forgive us. He chose to extend grace and offer us a second chance to be reconciled with Him.

Many of us find ourselves gradually consumed by anger and burdened with resentment due to the wounds we carry about. Moving forward becomes a daunting task, and rightfully so. Husbands, who should love their wives, have turned blind eyes to the deep wounds they've caused them. Fathers, who should be guiding their children towards godliness and purity, have turned into predators, sexually molesting their innocent kids. Mothers, expected to offer love and encouragement, have abandoned their homes and neglected their children during their crucial formative years. Friendships, once genuine and supportive, have transformed into arenas of slander and betrayal. Sincere apologies seem to be a rarity, leaving the wounds of psychological trauma raw and unhealed, akin to salt in an open wound.

These psychological traumas may linger, justifying our anger and resentment, but dwelling in them for prolonged periods can be detrimental to our well-being. Being kindled in anger is like being trapped in heavy shackles that prevent us from moving forward and hinder our spiritual growth. When anger takes root in our hearts, it becomes a constant reminder of past hurts and grievances, tethering us to the past and reliving the painful experiences over and over again. Forgiveness is God's gift to free us from the painful trap of backwardness when we experience hurt. It serves as a powerful tool that allows us to let go and move forward with renewed hope and healing. It is startling to see how much individualistic progress has been stifled because they could not move past anger. We find ourselves ensnared in the trap of waiting for retribution before we can extend forgiveness. The desire for the 'thief to face their punishment' holds our hearts captive and hinders our ability to let go of anger and resentment. At times, this desire for vengeance becomes so extreme that we wish harm upon people, believing it will bring us a sense of justification and peace before we can even consider forgiveness.

After Ammon had defiled Tamar, her brother Absalom was filled with rage and a burning desire to retaliate and avenge his sister's honor. Like Absalom, we may be filled with rage and seek revenge when we encounter justifiable discrepancies in our lives. It's impossible to not get angry sometimes when life throws us piercing thorns. Who wouldn't lose heart when it seems as if all their lives, they've constantly experienced the Titanic sinking? It is natural for someone who has faced one setback after another throughout their life – financial struggles, broken relationships, career setbacks, or health issues – and each blow feels like another hit to their already wounded heart, to question why they must endure such hardship or desire to see their oppressors face the consequences of their actions. The world gives us many reasons to feel angry, hurt, and want revenge but if we let ourselves be consumed by these negative emotions, we might miss the incredible transformation that forgiveness can bring.

If we clutch tightly to vengeance and retribution, we become blind to the steadfast anchor of forgiveness. It is not a swift eraser that wipes away the wrongs committed against us, nor does it instantly bestow a sense of justification or pacification. Forgiveness is sponsored by the fact that it is God's divine instruction to extend it to others, just as He has mercifully forgiven us. When we forgive others, we are doing what God has done for us many times. It's recognizing that we have also received God's limitless forgiveness. Instead of constantly looking for a good reason to forgive or waiting for the verdict of a court or the judgment of authorities, we take control and make the choice to forgive on our own, because ***Colossians 3:13 (NIV) urges us to "Bear with each other and forgive one another if any of you has a grievance against someone. Forgive as the Lord forgave you."*** As believers, forgiveness is no longer contingent on the recognition of wrongs or the acknowledgment of guilt. Rather, it springs forth from a place of respect and love for God who had already loved us and forgiven us. We grow above the natural inclination to retaliate and harbor grudges. We walk in the spirit (Gal 5:16), truly seated with Christ (Eph 2:6), emulating the example set by God, who, despite our imperfections and shortcomings, chose to love us and extend His forgiveness to us (Eph 5:1-2).

We know this because countless times throughout the Bible, we have been exhorted to forgive, not because our offenders necessarily deserve it, but because we, too, were once entangled in the miry clay of sin, with no hope for redemption. We were in a dark and troubled place, burdened by our sins but in the middle of our brokenness, mercy appeared, and we received the amazing gift of forgiveness, even when we didn't deserve it. Sometimes in our dealings, we may encounter individuals who resemble both the repentant thief on the cross with Jesus and the unrepentant and callous Jews who crucified Jesus. In such encounters, we are called to a remarkable standard — to exude kindness and compassion, extending forgiveness just as God forgave us through Christ's sacrificial love.

The ability to forgive others is deeply rooted in experiencing and understanding the love of God in our lives. When wounds run deep and the scars are too visible to let go, the idea of forgiveness can seem distant and quite challenging. Let's be honest, forgiveness is not an easy journey. It is only a heart that is flourishing in the experience of God's love that can be empowered to forgive. There are two folds to God's love. Firstly, the love that God has lavished on us is demonstrated by the giving of His only Son to die for our sins. Secondly, God's love stirred within our hearts and compelled us to walk in obedience. This love is the driving force behind our actions and decisions, guiding us to live a life that honors and glorifies Him. Love is powerful and it is more than fleeting feelings and emotions. It is a choice. A choice that is honored regardless of the perfections or imperfections of men. When we love people not because they are deserving, but because even in their worst states, God's grace does not abandon them to destruction. At the core of God's nature is a strong desire for even those who are deeply lost souls to find forgiveness and redemption. He deeply cares for those who have gone astray and tirelessly seeks ways to save them. Why would we want to hinder this mission? As lucky people who already have received the benevolence of God, why will our hearts be so hardened by resentment that we cannot be transformed by the love of God?

Many of us carry tightly locked hearts within us, fortified by walls of emotional barriers. This makes it challenging for anyone, even our dearest loved ones to tiptoe around us, knowing that the slightest misstep may invoke an irritable reaction. While we regularly confess our sins to God, seeking forgiveness when we wrong God, there's an important lesson from Jesus that we need to revisit. In ***Matthew 6 verse 14,*** Jesus says ***"For if you forgive others their trespasses, your heavenly Father will also forgive you, but if you do not forgive others their trespasses, neither will your Father forgive your trespasses."*** Jesus makes us understand that there is an interconnectedness between our experience of receiving forgiveness from God and our capacity to forgive others. It is not a transactional bargain but a spiritual law that governs the flow of grace and mercy. When we are faced with betrayal in friendships, business, or even within the bond of marriage, we are challenged to love in return. It is God's duty to heap the coals of fire on our enemies and not ours. When trust is shattered and loyalties are questioned, and the overwhelming desire for justice or revenge may arise, God wants us to entrust him with our pains, allowing us to feel lighter and capable of forgiving.

Moved by the Holy Spirit's guidance, Stephen had just delivered a sermon that pierced the heart of the high priest. The scriptures say, ***"When they heard these things, they were cut to the heart" (Acts 7:54 NKJV).*** However, instead of yielding to the stirring of the Holy Spirit, their hearts, hardened by pride and resistance, responded by stoning Stephen to death. Despite the torrent of hatred and injustice he faced, Stephen, like Jesus Christ, had a heart of forgiveness. Even as he lay battered and bruised, he cried out to God to forgive the high priests. In the face of adversity – even on the brink of death – we owe our enemies love and forgiveness. A forgiving heart may seem foolish in the eyes of the world. However, as followers of Christ, we are called to embody forgiveness, as exemplified by Jesus Himself and His disciples. In a world driven by pride and the desire for revenge, we are challenged to love not only our friends but also our enemies and to pray for those who persecute us (Mathew 5:44).

We mustn't burden others with the responsibility of healing the wounds they have inflicted on us. Even if they offer heartfelt apologies, the scars and pain may still linger. It is not within the capacity of human beings to mend crushing hearts and heal the brokenhearted. As such, it becomes counterproductive and draining to cling to the hurt and refuse to let go. It is only God who can truly mend the brokenhearted and save those who are crushed in spirit (Psalms 34:18).

One person that many of us struggle to forgive is ourselves. Satan, like a lion, prowls around, looking for someone to devour. He is constantly looking for any appearance of evil to keep us trapped in his shackles. He is the father of lies, capable of distorting the truth. This is the truth: ***"Jesus loves us and has freed us from our sins by His blood and made us a kingdom, priests to His God and Father, to him be glory and dominion forever and ever. Amen." (Rev 1:5b -6).***

When the guilt of the past hangs heavy on us and tempts us to doubt our worthiness of forgiveness, we must remember that the cross is the ultimate proof of God's love for us. "Who shall bring a charge against God's elect?" Nobody! Not even the cacophony of screaming voices in our heads or the haunting consequences of our past sins can condemn us. It hurts when your child resents you for the mistakes you made when you didn't know better. Even if you're in jail or trying hard to make things right, holding onto guilt won't help anyone, not even you. The heaviness of past, really bad mistakes shouldn't keep us trapped.

Think about it: What if Apostle Paul got stuck feeling guilty for his past as someone who harmed God's people? We might not remember that Paul used to go after Christians. He was involved in arresting and even killing believers. The mere mention of his name struck fear and trepidation in the hearts of those who followed the teachings of Jesus. But if he had stayed trapped in guilt, unable to believe he could go from persecuting Christians to passionately spreading the gospel, we would have missed out on the blessings of the Pauline epistles.

Give this scripture a read to understand how Paul managed to break free from his heavy past and follow the path God set for him. It's ***1st Timothy 1:15-16 (NLT), "This is a true saying, and everyone should believe it: Christ Jesus came into the world to save sinners, and I am the worst of them all. But God had mercy on me so that Christ Jesus could use me as a prime example of his great patience with even the worst sinners. Then others will realize that they, too, can believe***

in him and receive eternal life." Like Paul, we can let go of the past, forgive ourselves, and step into the new purpose God has for us.

As Christians, we tend to act a little funny! We have trouble fully accepting how deeply God forgives us, especially for those sins we think are worse. We're more comfortable believing God forgives the "normal" sins like lying or stealing. We might even rate sins on a scale and wonder if Jesus' sacrifice can wipe away the terrible ones. It's hard for us to accept that even if we admit and turn away from serious sins like murder, rape, or theft, God will truly forgive us, even if there are still consequences here on Earth. In ***Isaiah 1:18 (ESV)***, God invites us to talk it out, saying, ***"Come now, let's settle this, though your sins are like scarlet, I will make them as white as snow. Though they are red like crimson, I will make them as white as wool."*** Believe it, God can wash us clean, no matter how badly we've messed up.

Feeling guilty about our own mistakes can be just as strong, maybe even stronger, than struggling to forgive others. Don't let doubt and guilt planted by the devil cloud your thoughts and heart, stopping you from appreciating what God did for you through Jesus Christ. Remember this: ***"So now there is no condemnation for those who belong to Christ Jesus."*** That's ***Romans 8:1 (KJV).*** Quit being so hard on yourself for mistakes that even God has forgotten. Remember this: ***"So if the Son sets you free, you are truly free."*** Stay free! This isn't a temporary or halfway thing. It's freedom not only from past wrongs but also from guilt and shame. Even if others doubt your change, forgive yourself and keep on living the new way God's given you

Why Should We Forgive?

What happens when we refuse to forgive others and ourselves? Why should we forgive? Bitterness resides in our hearts when bonds of unforgiveness are tightly tied. The flames of resentment consume our souls when we cling to pain, refusing to let it go. Why should we hold onto grudges when forgiveness can mend what's torn and cold? Forgiveness impedes the joy and love that we all need; so why don't we release ourselves from this heavy chain and let God's mercy prevail?

These are some key reasons why we should forgive ourselves and others:

1. To Progress In God's Purpose For Our Lives

Once we let go of the weight of pain and grudges and find peace in God, we can move more freely on the path He planned for us. Just like David – he stayed strong on his way to becoming a king, even when Saul taunted and attacked him for no reason. Forgiving others lets us rise above the limits of our pain. It shifts our mindset. Instead of wanting payback, we tap into God's strength and wisdom. It helps us embrace God's purpose without being stuck in bitterness and anger.

2. To Sever The Roots Of Bitterness

Hebrews 12: 14 - 15 (NKJV) says, "Pursue peace with all people, and holiness, without which no one will see the Lord. Looking carefully lest anyone fall short of the grace of

God; lest any root of bitterness springing up cause trouble, and by this, many become defiled." Bitterness is a heavy emotional burden to bear, capable of keeping us stuck to the past and even unwarranted physical consequences. When bitterness takes root within us, it's as if a dense fog blankets our minds, obscuring our thoughts and emotions. As this bitterness festers, an overwhelming desire for revenge can take hold of us – not just for personal satisfaction, but also in the name of seeking justice. Satan takes advantage of this and begins to plant seeds of hatred in us toward others. In this state, it is easy to think of hurting or even killing others.

3. God Commands Us To Forgive

In the Lord's prayer, Jesus instructs His disciples to pray, ***"Forgive us our debts, as we also have forgiven our debtors"*** ***(Matthew 6:12 NIV).*** God has commanded us to forgive others for the wrongs they commit against us. If we love God we must demonstrate our obedience to all of his commandments, and that includes forgiving others. Also in ***Mark 11:25 -26 (NKJV)***, Jesus teaches us saying, ***"And whenever you stand praying, if you have anything against***

anyone, forgive him, that your Father in heaven may also forgive you your trespasses. But if you do not forgive, neither will your Father in heaven forgive your trespasses."

How Can We Be More Forgiving?

1. Surrender Your Heart To God

The heart is the cradle of all activities, especially when dealing with psychological affairs like forgiveness. Forgiving with a hardened heart is like felling a mahogany tree with a razor blade. If you find yourself being hard toward someone because of what they have done, there's no need to forgive with just your lips; instead, invite God into your heart and sincerely ask him to soften it with his love. If you cry sincerely to God, in Ezekiel 11:19, He promises to take the heart of stone out of your flesh and give you a heart of flesh.

2. Pray For Your Enemies

When we pray for our enemies, we begin to see them through God's eyes. We realize they're humans, loved by God, and needing His grace, just like us. Praying for them makes us understand their issues and hardships better. We begin to realize they might be hurting, insecure, or confused. Empathy makes forgiving them easier. When we pray for them, we ask God to help them with their struggles. Jesus tells us to do this in ***Matthew 5:43-45 (ESV)***; ***"You have heard that it was said, 'You shall love your neighbor and hate your enemy.' But I say to you, Love your enemies and pray for those who persecute you, so that you may be sons of your Father who is in heaven. For he makes his sun rise on the evil and the good and sends rain on the just and on the unjust."***

3. Determine to forgive in advance

Forgiving in advance is the attitude of peacemakers. Cut people some slack and realize that they are human beings who can hurt us sometimes. ***Romans 12:17 (NIV)*** encourages us to ***"not repay anyone evil for evil. Be careful to do what is right in the eyes of everyone. If it is possible, as far as it depends on you, live at peace with everyone."*** When Jesus said we should forgive seventy times seven times, He implied that we should have an arsenal of forgiveness. Once we recognize a hurt or an offense, do not wait for an apology. Do what God has commanded us to do.

CHAPTER EIGHT

Cultivating Contentment

Now godliness with contentment is a great gain. For we brought nothing into this world, and it is certain we can carry nothing out. And having food and clothing, with these we shall be content. But those who desire to be rich fall into temptation and a snare, and into many foolish and harmful lusts which drown men in destruction and perdition. The love of money is a root of all kinds of evil, for which some have strayed from the faith in their

greediness, and pierced themselves through with many sorrows. (1st Timothy 6:6-10 NKJV)

Are you caught in the whirlwind of life, constantly striving for success, and overlooking the simple joys of today? In this fast-paced world, it's easy to get lost in the pursuit of bigger achievements while forgetting to cherish the blessings we already have. Do you find yourself fixated on waiting for that one big breakthrough, missing the little answered prayers that could make your today beautiful? Life is a breathtaking gift from God, meant to be embraced and lived to the fullest. Yet, the pressure to achieve more, to always be reaching for new heights, can leave us exhausted and discontented.

The book of Philippians, chapter four, is an intriguing read. In this chapter, Paul emphasizes rejoicing in the Lord. If the neighbors herald new cars every season and all you have got is to jump on trains and cabs, you rejoice in the Lord. Paul speaks as if the hustle to meet up and make a statement is completely irrelevant. While they make their boast and rejoice in their horses and chariots, new rides and toys, you rejoice in the Lord. It is still in this beautiful chapter that he implores us to be anxious for nothing. A lot of us are enduring heightened anxiety issues because our clamor for material status and societal approval is outrageous. Believers are caught in a frenzied chase! Marital relationships suffer and are strained when partners become upset and disappointed with each other for not fulfilling their material fantasies. Similarly, kids might act out after hanging out with richer friends, not respecting their parents anymore. What have we turned into while chasing our desires? What have we done to make things fancier? We've become obsessed with wanting more. Our simple search for basic needs has been replaced with a focus on luxury and excess. You'd be surprised to see what people do to show off wealth and status.

Discontentment in the life of a Christian is a stark indication of misplaced priorities. It shows that our focus has shifted from seeking the kingdom of God and His righteousness (Mathew 6:33) to chasing after the fleeting pleasures of life. It is an attempt to take matters into our hands as if God is incapable or slow in launching us into our season of abundance. The Israelites made this mistake during their journey to the promised land. Looking at the way Paul put it in ***Philippians 4:11 (NIV)***, he said; ***"I have learned to be content whatever the circumstances."*** Well, despite enduring the hardships inflicted by the Egyptians and fervently praying for God's deliverance, the Israelites still couldn't reach the promised land due to their constant discontentment. They could not learn that the same God who saved them from their enemies could provide them with enough food and stuff for their journey. They began to demand irrelevant things from God and lost sight of His capacity to provide. They even began to accuse God of hating them because their journey was filled with thorns and thistles. Discontentment makes us lose sight of all that God has done for us and judge Him as unfaithful.

You might wonder, what's wrong with desiring a better life and aiming for the skies? Wouldn't living lavishly and abundantly be a reflection of God's goodness toward us? Wanting a better life or aiming for success and abundance isn't wrong by itself. God has placed dreams and ambitions within us, and He delights in seeing us thrive and grow. He wants to bless us and provide for our needs, and there's nothing sinful about living a beautiful and fulfilling life. However, the real concern is the attitude behind these desires.

When our pursuit of a better life becomes an obsession for material possessions, status, and worldly achievements, it becomes a problem. It becomes a problem when we can comfortably disobey God, complain, and grumble if God hasn't met any of our demands. ***1st Timothy 6:9 (NKJV)*** makes us understand that ***"those who desire to be rich fall into temptation and a snare, and into many foolish and harmful lusts which drown men in destruction and perdition. For the love of money is a root of all kinds of evil, for which some have strayed from the faith in their greediness, and pierced themselves through with many sorrows."***

People who aren't content end up relying on money instead of God. Money becomes their source of joy. You can see it when they get a fat paycheck and when things go bad. Riches become their idols and the basis of their happiness. They are enslaved to the spirit of mammon, and soon they will have to choose between serving God or mammon. A man allows himself to be a slave serving mammon when he refuses to acknowledge that the seasons of lack and struggles in his life are not entirely about his struggles. It's about him and his trust in God. If you look forward to being planted by the riverside with your leaves springing forth in due season, you should also be expectant of the hands of the Lord guiding you through the valley of the shadow of death.

God deeply despises discontentment because it not only limits His work in our lives but also implies that we view Him merely as a means to fulfill our selfish desires. A lot of us just treat God as a vending machine, expecting immediate gratification to satisfy our every whim. When a man comes to God, the foundational class God puts him through is the need to depend completely on Him. God wants us to lay down our agendas, relinquish control, and rely solely on Him.

In Luke 12:13-21, Jesus narrates the parable of the rich fool to teach us the dangers of discontentment and the need to cultivate contentment as believers. Jesus warns us to "beware of covetousness, for one's life does not consist in the abundance of things we possess." In simple terms, our true worth and happiness cannot be measured by the size of our possessions. We could have the fanciest houses with amazing rooms, but at the end of the day, when things quiet down, we're still sleeping in just one room. Material wealth can deceive us with the illusion of peace and treasure, tempting us to covet more out of discontentment. Yet, in reality, this pursuit is futile and foolish. It is like chasing after a mirage in the desert, always seeking something just out of reach.

Once, a wealthy man prepared for a journey to a far-off land. Before leaving, he summoned his household servants and entrusted them with some investment capital. To the first servant, he gave five dollars; to the second, he gave two dollars; and to the third, he gave one dollar. The first two servants diligently set out to trade with the resources their master had given them. With contentment and focus, they multiplied their investments, reaping profits as they worked diligently. When the master returned from his journey, he found these two servants faithful and successful in managing his resources. But the third servant acted differently. Instead of seizing the opportunity to invest and grow what he was given, he got upset and bitter. He looked at what the others got and felt like he deserved more. He didn't see the worth in even the one talent he had, seeing it as less important than the rest. Sadly, the third servant's reaction was full of laziness and gripes. Instead of working with what he was given, he buried his talent in the ground and refused to take any risks or responsibility. This is the parable of the talent that Jesus made in Matthew 25:14-30. Discontentment makes us approach the gifts God has bestowed on us with the attitude of the third servant. We desire more, yet the seeds in our garden remain untended, dismissed as insignificant. Our preoccupation with our deficiencies blinds us to the potential abundance surrounding us. Our hearts are hurried, driven to chase after what others possess.

Sadly, there are consequences for not being faithful to what God gives us. In the parable of the talent, when the master came back, he held each servant accountable for their actions. He commended the first two for their faithfulness and rewarded them with greater responsibilities and blessings. Contentment holds the key to unlocking doors of greater opportunities and blessings in our lives because we have acknowledged that God knows what is best for us and has equipped us with the exact resources we need for our journey. Did you know that once God sees our complete dependence on Him, He becomes moved to do more just so our Faith in Him grows stronger? He takes pleasure in surprising us with His grace and exceeding our expectations. Parents might struggle to fully appreciate the trust and faith their children have in them to provide for their needs, especially when resources are limited. However, God, who is the owner of all riches, perceives and values the sincere trust we place in Him. He stands ready to disburse His abundance to meet our needs and shower us with even more blessings, once He sees our contentment with the little He provides each day.

The master rebuked the third servant who was not profitable with the little amount he was given. The reward for discontentment is in ***Matthew 25:28-29 (NKJV) "So take the talent from him, and give it to him who has ten talents. For to everyone who has, more will be given, and he will have abundance; but from him who does not have, even what he has will be taken away."*** When we don't appreciate what God has given us and fail to use our resources wisely, we cut ourselves off from the flow of His blessings. Like this unfaithful servant who buried his talent and compared himself to others who were endowed with more, our discontentment hinders us from experiencing the abundance God desires to pour into our lives. The reward for discontentment is that we remain stagnant, unable to grow or make progress. We become stuck in a cycle of dissatisfaction and unfulfillment. The little in our hands can slip through our fingers, leaving us with even less.

In today's world, lots of people could be excited about the idea of interning with someone like Prophet Elisha. They'd want to see and learn from the amazing things God might be doing through him. It's like having a front-row seat to witness those miracles up close and personal. However, what we do not know is if we could have done better than Gehazi, who succumbed to the lure of greed and coveted more than his master permitted. When Elisha turned down the fancy gifts that Naaman, the Syrian commander, wanted to give him, Gehazi saw his chance to satisfy his wants. What Gehazi did showed that he wasn't happy with the simple and dedicated life he had while working with Elisha. It's like he wanted more than what he had, even though he was already in a good place. We struggle so hard to reach great heights and attain worldly success that we often find ourselves scorched by the searing heat of our ambitions. We might have our eyes set on things we believe we want, like impressive accomplishments and stuff, but it's only God who sees the dangers of chasing after wealth and popularity when it's not the right time or way. Just check out what happened to Gehazi – his story is pretty sad. Instead of becoming a respected prophet in Israel, he ended up getting leprosy. It shows how things can go wrong when we don't go along with God's timing and the way He provides for us.

When discontentment is planted in our hearts, it yields the fruit of greed and covetousness. At first, it may seem like a harmless emotion; however, if left unchecked, it can gradually transform into an insatiable craving for possessions, power, and recognition. We become like a bottomless pit, always wanting more, and never finding true satisfaction in what we have been given. In our dissatisfaction, we begin to covet what belongs to others; we even resent them for having what we desire. This is what happened to the Devil. He got all fired up with pride and wanting more, so he went against God and went from being a respected angel in heaven to being God's biggest enemy. When we allow discontentment to rule our hearts, we risk losing sight of what truly matters – our relationship with God and the genuine contentment that comes from knowing and serving Him.

Contentment is knowing that ***"life is more than food and the body is more than clothing" (Luke 12:23).*** It is having an understanding that the presence, power, and glory of God can manifest not only through precious metals like gold or silver but also through humble earthen vessels and ordinary, base things of this world. Even though the world values being rich, even if we're not all that fancy, God might still decide to be with us and work through us. The contentment path is like carrying the Savior of the world until it's the right time for Him to show up. It's about being okay with bringing Him into the world, even if the place is super humble – like a basic barn that stinks because of animals. You wouldn't think a king or any child would be born there, but that's where it happened. Contentment means being sure that if God has clearly said "Yes," then we don't have to go and do shady stuff like bribes, tricks, or illegal things to make His plans happen. Even when things are tough or we don't have much, we believe that God will step in and make things work out the way He wants, no matter what.

The reality of our Christian life is that we cannot pursue perfection outside of God. Any endeavor to improve ourselves, conceal our flaws, and achieve certain standards without relying on God and His grace will ultimately be tainted and flawed. It is already a corrupted approach. The desire for more was planted inside of us by God. It isn't strange that for each mark we attain, we revel and celebrate it for a while; then wake up with another void, a greater and deeper longing to pursue more. It is a craving for more that can only be satisfied within the sufficiency of God's presence. Attempting to fill this gap with things from the world and believing we can manage everything on our own is akin to engaging in sexual activity outside of marriage – it won't lead to a successful outcome. We'll ultimately miss the mark.

How To Cultivate Contentment

1. Be At Peace With Your Insufficiencies

Do you know about the serenity prayer? It is a popular prayer founded on Biblical principles. The first part of the serenity prayer says ***"God grant me the serenity to accept the things I cannot change…"*** To build a culture of contentment, it is really important to make peace with the things we cannot change. When we do this, we start seeing that these unchangeable aspects of our lives serve as conduits through which God makes bold statements in our lives. Contentment does not imply complacency, but rather a peace that comes from faith in God's providence, despite our flaws. Paul demonstrates this perfectly with the statement he made in *2 Corinthians 12:9-10 (NKJV)*; ***"And He said to me, 'My grace is sufficient for you, for My strength is made perfect in weakness.' Therefore most gladly I will rather boast in my infirmities, that the power of Christ may rest upon me. Therefore I take pleasure in infirmities, in reproaches, in needs, in persecutions, in distresses, for Christ's sake. For when I am weak, then I am strong."*** It is best to believe that our irreversible insufficiencies and weaknesses are not powerful enough to stop us from enjoying God's blessings for us. There's no need to engage in all sorts of unimaginable things to change what you should be content with.

2. Trust In God's Sufficiency and Providence

God doesn't need us to have certain abilities to provide for us. He's not sitting around waiting for us to be rich, powerful, or well-connected before He makes the doors He wants us to walk through open up. His plans for us aren't held back by how things are or what we have. When God sets a path for us, He's ahead of us, making the way clear and getting everything ready for each step of our journey. Let us look at the Prophecy of Elisha to King Jehoshaphat in ***2nd Kings 3:17(NKJV), "Thus says the LORD: 'Make this valley full of ditches.' For thus says the LORD: 'You shall not see wind, nor shall you see rain; yet that valley shall be filled with water, so that you, your cattle, and your animals may drink."*** How do you fathom a dry and barren valley being filled with water, especially without the visible signs of wind or rain? Filled enough for cattle and other animals to drink? Believe the fact that God has more than enough resources to bless us with. Even when we can't see it, He's got plenty of resources to provide for us. God can change our tough situations into sources of great blessings. We don't need to feel jealous or want what others have. If God tells you to take brave steps and get ready, even if things look tough and unclear, don't go crazy trying to find money and stuff to make it work. Stick to what He gives you to work with.

Philippians 4:19-20 assures us that all we shall ever need will be provided to us according to God's riches in Glory. Our response to this is to trust God. Get rid of haste and trust that God can do what He deems perfect for you.

3. Rejoicing In God Irrespective Of The Outcomes

Habakkuk 3:17–19 (NKJV) says ***"Though the fig tree should not blossom, nor fruit be on the vines, the produce of the olive fail and the fields yield no food, the flock is cut off from the fold and there be no herd in the stalls, yet I will rejoice in the LORD; I will take joy in the God of my salvation. God, the Lord, is my strength; he makes my feet like the deer's; he makes me tread on my high places."*** These signs show a city or economy that's failing and going backward. It's when everything you do doesn't give good results. Even if you work hard but don't get much back, or you put time and stuff into things and they don't work out well, and you're let down by different things you try – Habakkuk's response to this is to still find joy in God. A heart of gratitude is important. It's like saying, 'Hey, God's in charge here, and He's making everything work out fine for us, even when things look tough.' It's about recognizing that even in difficult times, God's got a plan. Instead of getting all negative, grumbling, and saying bad things because of what's happening now, try having a thankful attitude. To be grateful, we need to see the good even when things are hard. Instead of focusing on what we lack, we should value the small moments of happiness and good things we usually miss. In Philippians 4:6-7 (NIV), Paul encourages us: "Do not be anxious about anything but in every situation, by prayer and petition, with thanksgiving, present your requests to God. And the peace of God, which transcends all understanding, will guard your hearts and your minds in Christ Jesus."

4. Get Rid Of Comparison

Getting rid of comparison is a powerful way to cultivate contentment in our lives. It is natural for us to look at others and compare what they have with what we lack, and this breeds envy and discontentment in us. In ***1st Corinthians 7:17 (ESV),*** Paul tells us ***"Only let each person lead the life***

that the Lord has assigned to him, and to which God has called him…" Sadly, comparison makes us lose sight of what God called us into. We may think that we should be doing what they are doing or achieving what they have achieved. We overlook the beautiful plan that God has specifically designed for us. He may not have called us to be the highest donor in church, but his gift of wisdom to us can also move the church forward. Recognize that God's calling for each individual is tailor-made, and He equips us with unique gifts and abilities to fulfill that calling.

Hebrews 13:5 (NKJV) says ***"Keep your life free from love of money, and be content with what you have, for he has said, 'I will never leave you nor forsake you."*** There is peace in contentment where we can rest from unnecessary worries and bask in true riches in God.

CHAPTER NINE

The Pursuit of Wisdom

"Do not forsake wisdom, and she will protect you; love her, and she will watch over you. The beginning of wisdom is this: Get wisdom. Though it costs all you have, get understanding." (Proverbs 4:6-7 NIV).

God's wisdom is what we can count on to make good choices, discern right from wrong, and live by God's will. In this dynamic and ever-changing race called life, it is the beacon that guides us through the labyrinth of decisions, challenges, and experiences. Like how an experienced traveler changes their compass based on the different landscapes, we also need wisdom that suits our particular times and situations. It's a bit like how a river flows around obstacles in its path. Wisdom helps us adapt, switch our course, and beat the obstacles that pop up on our journey. It helps us know if we should hit the rock with a rod or simply talk to it. These two actions don't lead to the same outcome, but wisdom helps us understand which one is what God wants us to do.

The call for wisdom is one that a Christian dares not ignore; because to miss this call is to venture on a perilous journey that is filled with pitfalls and death traps. Life itself is a maze of darkness with lots of wrong turns and misleading paths. Relying solely on our own or the world's wisdom is like carrying dim lanterns that will lead to a bad outcome. Those lanterns might give off some light, but they're like feeble candles struggling in a strong wind. They can only show a fraction of the road ahead, leaving much of it in the dark. Relying on just our smarts can take us only so far. As we get older and approach the end of our lives, we grasp this truth: our smarts start to fade. Like the wise virgins in Jesus' parable, only those who truly seek and treasure God's wisdom manage to triumph in life.

God's wisdom is the strategy given to us to navigate and win here on Earth. If God wanted us to lean solely on our human reasoning, He certainly would not have given us this warning in ***Proverbs 3:7a (ESV), "Be not wise in your own eyes..."*** God, who created us, did indeed give us the capacity for sound judgment and smart decisions. However, He cautions against leaning solely on our understanding. Why? Because human understanding is limited and can sometimes lead us astray due to our own biases, misunderstandings, and incomplete perspectives. God's guidance helps us navigate life with a broader and more complete view, preventing us from getting lost in our assumptions and potentially harmful choices. Our bodies are about seventy percent water, which shows how crucial water is for life. It's the same for all living things – water is essential to stay alive, support growth, and maintain balance. But even though water is so important, we wouldn't want to drink sewage water or water from a really dirty stream. It's not safe. Even plants suffer and die if they're watered with water that has too much sodium. The wisdom we naturally have isn't as pure as the wisdom described in the scriptures when talking about God's wisdom. ***James 3:17-18 (ESV)*** says, ***"But the wisdom from above is first pure, then peaceable, gentle, open to reason, full of mercy and good fruits, impartial and sincere. And a harvest of righteousness is sown in peace by those who make peace."*** Unlike God's wisdom, human wisdom is a bit complicated. It can be influenced by what we like, how we feel, and what society tells us. It's a bit like water with too much sodium – it might seem okay, but it doesn't give us what we need for a successful spiritual journey. If we rely solely on our thoughts, we might overlook crucial details, misinterpret situations, or make choices based on our desires rather than what's truly best.

Samuel had the task of picking the next king for Israel. The plan was clear: one of Jesse's sons would be the king, and Samuel had to find the right one and anoint him. As each son was brought before him, Samuel's judgment was kind of influenced by his wisdom. He kept noticing the ones who looked tall, strong, and like they had the royal vibe. It matched the common idea that looking impressive on the outside meant being fit to be a king. But the thing is, Samuel didn't realize that human smarts might value things that God sees as normal. God's wisdom is above what we usually think and see.

Remember, in this chapter, when we mention working and achieving things with wisdom, we're talking about the real wisdom that comes from above. This wisdom is like a sure light for our path, preventing us from tripping and falling.

Wisdom is beyond mere knowledge or just collating facts and information. It is truly understanding the complicated parts of life and how we can advance to create a world that is filled with the glory of the Lord. After the devil had been cast into the earth, our ecosystem has been doused in darkness and wickedness; but God has given us His wisdom to dispel darkness and counteract the influences of the devil. This shows how crucial wisdom is to us.

Proverbs 16:16 (ESV) says ***"How much better to get wisdom than gold! To get understanding is to be chosen rather than silver."*** The bible prices wisdom above gold. Gold is not very common in nature, so there's not a lot of it – because it's not easy to find, it's considered valuable – people are willing to pay more for it. Gold is super valuable because it doesn't rust or corrode. This means it stays beautiful and precious for a long time. But the Bible says that God's wisdom is even better than gold, which has captivated people for ages with its charm. God's wisdom is always there and never changes, even when time goes by. It can still help and do amazing things, even save people.

In a myriad of choices and conflicting paths, God's wisdom teaches us the right way to walk. In Psalms 32:8, God assures us that He will instruct us and teach us in the way we should go. He says He will counsel us with His loving eyes. Just as a loving parent instructs a child, God takes an active role in imparting wisdom, helping us understand the choices before us. The assurance of God's ***"loving eye"*** means He is always there, watching over us. God doesn't just give us wisdom and direction when we're unsure about which path to take; His guidance is with us every step of the way. We can trust that He's always there, so we're not alone when we face life's difficulties.

Why We Need Wisdom

1. Dealing With Life's Difficulties

Life is filled with challenges, uncertainties, and dilemmas and God's wisdom is the foolproof approach we need to navigate through this messy maze of life. When Joseph was faced with the daunting challenge of interpreting Pharaoh's dreams about seven years of plenty followed by seven years of famine. With God's wisdom, Joseph accurately interpreted the dreams and provided a plan to save Egypt and the surrounding regions. In 1st Kings 3, Solomon was faced with a dire situation where two women claimed the same child as their own. With God's wisdom, he came up with a test that revealed the true mother's identity and resolved the matter justly. We can surely bank on God's wisdom to bail us out. Moreover, ***Proverbs 3:21-23 (NIV)*** says, ***"My son, do not let wisdom and understanding out of your sight, preserve sound judgment and discretion; they will be life for you, an ornament to grace your neck. Then you will go on your way in safety, and your foot will not stumble."*** This is the promise that even when things get chaotic and tough, God's wisdom will help us stay strong and make the right choices, guiding us on the right track.

2. For Safety And Preservation:

Proverbs 2:12 (ESV) says ***"Wisdom will save you from the ways of wicked men, from men whose words are perverse..."*** God's wisdom makes us strong against the wiles of wickedness. It empowers us to say no to things that might lead us the wrong way. It gives us the power to stay strong when things test our sense of what's right and wrong. In a time when there are lots of misleading ideologies, our only measure of truth and value is God's wisdom. A man who is not subscribed to God's wisdom has positioned himself to be swallowed up by Satan's deceptive traps. That person becomes vulnerable to tricky and evil lies. Proverbs 2:20 shows that God's wisdom can help us stay in goodness and righteousness. God doesn't want Christians whose beliefs and moral stand are swayed by the changing trends of society. He wants us to surrender to His wisdom, staying firm in Him and His values.

3. Material Success and Wealth:

It is God's desire for us to be rich and wealthy. Here is what ***Isaiah 48:17(NKJV)*** says: ***"...I am the LORD your God, Who teaches you to profit, Who leads you by the way you should go." Deuteronomy 8:18 (NKJV)*** also states, ***"And you shall remember the Lord your God, for it is He who gives you the power to get wealth."*** When the Bible says that God gives us the power to create wealth, it means He is the ultimate source of our abilities. The wisdom of God can inspire novel and ground-breaking ideas that fetch us wealth. Godly wisdom can lead us to ideas that are not only innovative but also morally and ethically sound. This ensures that our creative expressions contribute to the betterment of society. When our ideas are inspired by God's wisdom, they can address real-world needs and challenges. This purpose-driven innovation has the potential to attract attention, create value, and lead to financial success. The wisdom of God has the power to elevate our ideas beyond personal success to a broader impact. This was the testimony of King Solomon in 2 Chronicles 9:23-24 (ESV): "And all the kings of the earth sought the presence of Solomon to hear his wisdom, which God had put into his mind. Every one of them brought his present, articles of silver and gold, garments, myrrh, spices, horses, and mules, so much year by year.

How To Pursue Wisdom In Our Daily Life And Grow In Discernment

The first box you must tick in your desire for God's wisdom is to surrender yourself to God's government. ***Proverbs 2:6 (NIV) opens a window into the wellspring of wisdom: "For the Lord gives wisdom; from his mouth comes knowledge and understanding."*** Wisdom isn't just an idea or something people create. It is a special gift from God, coming directly from who God is. If we are going to be led by God's wisdom, we must first surrender to God with a sense of fear and reverence. ***Proverbs 1:7 (NIV) says: "The fear of the Lord is the beginning of knowledge, but fools despise wisdom and instruction."*** Fear doesn't simply mean being afraid in a negative sense, but rather showing deep respect, reverence, and awe for God's authority and wisdom. It means submitting and bringing all aspects of your life to the obedience of God's wisdom which is very evident in the scriptures. It's through this posture of humility and reverence that we become receptive to His wisdom and instruction.

When you surrender to God and make his words the final authority over your life, you can ask God for the spirit of wisdom. This is the second box to check. ***James 1:5-6 (NIV) says "If any of you lacks wisdom, you should ask God, who gives generously to all without finding fault, and it will be given to you. But when you ask, you must believe and not doubt, because the one who doubts is like a wave of the sea, blown and tossed by the wind."*** There will be times when we lack the wisdom to navigate dire situations or make important choices. In such moments, James encourages us to turn to God and seek His wisdom through prayer. Unlike humans who might be hesitant to share knowledge or might find fault with our requests, when we earnestly ask God for wisdom, it will be granted. This doesn't mean that God will necessarily reveal all the future details, but He will provide the insight, discernment, and understanding needed to move ahead.

When you have these two foundational fountains of God's wisdom checked, then do the following consistently:

- Study and meditate on the scriptures.
- Pray often.
- Seek wise counsel.
- Cultivate a teachable spirit.
- Reflect and evaluate your actions regularly with the word of God.

The pursuit of wisdom is not a solitary endeavor; it's a collaborative dance between our hearts and God's eternal wisdom. By surrendering, seeking, and consistently engaging in practices that nurture our understanding, we enter a realm where wisdom becomes a guiding light, leading us through the complexities of life. May these principles and practices resonate within you, shaping a life steeped in God's wisdom and filled with discernment.

CHAPTER TEN

Walking with Purpose

"Before I formed you in the womb I knew you, before you were born I set you apart; I appointed you as a prophet to the nations." (Jeremiah 1:5 NIV)

God has a specific purpose for every one of us. Psalm 139:13-16 emphasizes that God knits us together in the womb and ordains our days. This means that our existence is not accidental; we are intentionally designed by God for a purpose. The purpose is defined as the reason for which something is created or exists, often implying a particular intention, goal, or role. For us, as God's creation, purpose is beyond mere existence; it encompasses God's divine plan or calling that each individual is meant to fulfill during their lifetime. The purpose is the reason we were brought into being, the role we are uniquely equipped to play in God's grand narrative.

It's a big mistake to think we're just here on Earth without any real reason. Our presence here is far from co-incidental so not thinking about why we're here is like missing an important part of being human. This question of "why" is really important. It can change how we go through life, decide things, and make our lives more meaningful. Purpose fosters a sense of responsibility—an understanding that our actions ripple through the lives of those around us. It's a call to contribute, to leave a legacy that extends beyond our existence.

God's purpose for our lives goes beyond the ambitions and aspirations that occupy our thoughts. It goes beyond the aims we work towards and the things we want. While these are important and can make us excited, they're just parts of a bigger plan God has entrusted us with. Most times, God's purpose for our lives may elevate us beyond our expectations and leave us astounded. His purpose can surpass the boundaries of our wildest dreams, catching us off guard and evoking a sense of disbelief in us. ***Jeremiah 1:4-6 (ESV); "Now the word of the Lord came to me, saying, 'Before I formed you in the womb I knew you, and before you were born I consecrated you; I appointed you a prophet to the nations.' Then I said, 'Ah, Lord God! Behold, I do not know how to speak, for I am only a youth."*** We see here that when God called the Prophet Jeremiah and unveiled His purpose for his life, His initial reaction was to point out his inadequacy and unworthiness. He wondered how he could function in the shoes of a prophet to the nation of Israel. When God unveils His purpose for our lives, He isn't necessarily anticipating us to possess the complete skill set and readiness for the path He lays before us. Instead, His desire is for us to walk alongside Him, maintaining our connection with Him, as He gradually equips us to fulfill

His calling. Just like Jeremiah felt he wasn't ready for the big job he was given, we might also feel like we're not enough for what God wants us to do. But it's important to know that when God asks us to do something, He also promises to help us and give us all we need for an excellent job.

Walking with Purpose is a call to actively contribute to the expansion of God's Kingdom. God created us as vessels and in *2 Timothy 2:20-21,* the Bible tells us: ***"But in a great house there are not only vessels of gold and silver but also wood and clay, some for honor and some for dishonor. Therefore if anyone cleanses himself from the latter, he will be a vessel for honor, sanctified and useful for the Master, prepared for every good work."*** Every individual born into this world is a vessel. Our lives carry the potential to convey content that either contributes to the edification of God's Kingdom or aligns with the agenda of the adversary. Your vessel also can harbor self-centered desires and ambitions, where your focus narrows down to your wants and aspirations — your attention becomes fixated solely on pursuing your agenda.

A vessel has the liberty to choose the nature of its content, either for honor or dishonor. If we aim to walk in purpose, aligning ourselves with God's desires and becoming diligent workers who earn the approval of our Master, it becomes imperative to purge ourselves of every load: whether it's the weight of selfish tendencies, the stagnation of laziness, the delay caused by procrastination, or the entanglement of sin.

Our admiration is often drawn towards a meticulously shaped and elegantly pruned flower, a stark contrast to the wild and untamed growth of shrubs. Similarly, the concept of God's freedom, bestowed upon us through the sacrifice of Jesus on the cross, is undeniably beautiful. However, this freedom doesn't imply a life of unbridled abandon. Our lives should not resemble the unruly nature of wild shrubs! Our lives find their true form and flourish when guided by purpose. Purpose guides us to follow God's plan for us. It makes us focus our energy and dreams in the right direction. It helps us think, act, and want things that fit with what God wants for us. This way, our lives are more thoughtful and not chaotic. Paul implied this in ***1st Corinthians 9:26***

(NIV), "Therefore I do not run like someone running aimlessly; I do not fight like a boxer beating the air." Purpose unveils what truly matters, helping us focus our attention on the vital aspects of life while filtering out distractions.

Knowing Your Purpose In God

Knowing our purpose from God isn't about just following what others do or going after temporary trends. It's about finding a plan that's made just for us — a plan that isn't made by what people think but by God's careful design. The Bible tells us this in ***Isaiah 55:8-9 (NIV), "For my thoughts are not your thoughts, neither are your ways my ways," declares the Lord. "As the heavens are higher than the earth, so are my ways higher than your ways and my thoughts than your thoughts."*** Ephesians 2:10 (NIV) complements this by saying: "For we are God's handiwork, created in Christ Jesus to do good works, which God prepared in advance for us to do." So we do not just follow what we desire or what others expect of us, the best place where our spiritual sensitivity is heightened to discern God's purpose for our lives is in the place of prayer. When we constantly fellowship with God through prayers, the loud voices of our spirits quiet down and we begin to perceive with more clarity what God wants us to do. It is important to be led by the Holy Spirit through prayers, meditation, and a surrendered heart.

Whatever God has revealed to us in the place of prayer must conform to and advance the original commission that God has entrusted into the care of every believer in ***Matthew 18:19-20 (NIV): "Therefore go and make disciples of all nations, baptizing them in the name of the Father and of the Son and the Holy Spirit, and teaching them to obey everything I have commanded you. And surely I am with you always, to the very end of the age."*** Finding our individual life purpose is part of the bigger picture of making God's Kingdom grow. Our purpose isn't meant to take us away from the main task of spreading God's message, but to make our work in it even better. It's like a thread that fits perfectly into God's plan to make things right, making it even better and stronger.

What To Do After Discovering Your Purpose

One of the tragic incidents recorded in the Bible is in ***Acts 1:20 (ESV): "...may his camp become desolate, and let there be no one to dwell in it and let another take his office."*** Peter made this statement concerning Judas Iscariot, though one of the twelve Apostles, and was a key mastermind in the death of Jesus Christ. The lesson here is clear: what we do with the purpose revealed to us carries immense weight. Our response to God's calling can either ignite the flames of passion, growth, and impact, as Paul advised Timothy in 2 Timothy 1:6, or it can lead us down a path of indiscipline, wasted potential, and missed opportunities. Paul advised Timothy to fan into flame the gift of God that was given to him. After discovering your purpose in the place of prayers, here are a couple of things you can do so your profiting can appear to others, especially to God;

1. Total Dedication And Commitment

One of the plagues of our generation is our half-hearted and lackadaisical approach to things of significance. We don't put all our effort, attention, and commitment into things we need to do. This happens in different parts of life, like how we relate to others, work, improve ourselves, and follow our spiritual path. We are a distracted generation with an insatiable desire for instant gratification. When God gives us a purpose, it's like putting a seed in the ground – a seed with the potential to grow big and have a big effect. But like a seed needs time, care, and the right conditions to grow, our purpose also needs time to develop. This is a crucial time when we need to build the qualities, skills, and character needed for our purpose to start and grow. However, this is also when we might get tired and distracted. The promise of quick results and success can make us stop focusing on our purpose. The world offers things that seem good, but they can lead us away from patiently working on our purpose. For our purpose to find full expression, we must be dedicated and sold out to it. We must approach as Jesus did with the mission of salvation and redemption that God gave to Him.

2. Work with a sense of urgency

God's business requires haste, especially in the times we live in. We cannot afford to procrastinate and lazy around because the Devil is working very hard to trap more souls into his bondage. ***In John 9:4 (ESV),*** Jesus tells us ***"We must work the works of him who sent me while it is day; night is coming when no one can work."*** Working with a sense of urgency means understanding that every moment is full of possibility. It's choosing to put God's mission first, even when things try to take your attention away. Like a runner speeding toward the end of a race, you need to work faster, knowing that now is the time to make a big difference.

3. Be Courageous

When Joshua succeeded Moses, God repeatedly encouraged him to be strong and courageous. A lot of us may be robbed of the joy of walking in our purpose because of fear. When we're faced with things that make us uncomfortable, it's normal to feel fear. But fear becomes a problem when it stops us from moving. It shows up as not believing in ourselves, feeling worried, and thinking we're not good enough. This can make us stuck and afraid. God has not given us a spirit of fear, He expects and even commands us to be courageous. When we begin to walk on purpose we will surely encounter a lot of ugly situations simply because the light we shine threatens them. Let's see what God commanded Jeremiah to do in ***Jeremiah 1:8 (ESV): "Do not be afraid of them, for I am with you to deliver you…*** *"*Yes! God has commanded us to be courageous in what He has called us to do for His Kingdom.

Purpose, beyond a mere notion, is the guiding force that directs our journey through life. It's the compass that points us toward our unique roles in God's grand narrative. As we've explored, it's easy to overlook this purpose amidst the hustle and bustle of everyday life. Yet, recognizing our purpose isn't just an abstract endeavor—it's a transformative quest that imbues our lives with deeper meaning and intentionality.

Our purpose, intricately woven into God's grand design, is an essential thread in the tapestry of His Kingdom's expansion. It's not a solitary pursuit but a harmonious symphony that resonates with the melody of God's divine purpose. So, let us walk this path with courage, embracing our purpose as a divine calling to impact the world as vessels of God's purpose and grace.

CONCLUSION

In the captivating journey through the chapters of "Foolproof," we've explored the intricate details of our lives, uncovering hidden aspects and confronting the complexities of being human. Throughout the themes in this book, a strong message rang out – we should bring our struggles, fears, and negative behaviors to God's throne of grace. The metaphorical "closet space" showed us the weight of secrets, shame, and the need for honesty in our relationship with God. By embracing God's love, forgiveness, wisdom, and purpose, we aren't just watching – we're part of God's plan to make things right. When we let go of keeping secrets and being scared, we're reborn into lives full of faith, happiness, and deep joy.

This is the message that fills the pages of "Foolproof." Satan has no hold over us when we let go of bitterness and resentment. His demonic bond is severed forever as we choose to align with God's wisdom for every season of our lives. Most importantly, we depopulate the Kingdom of darkness when we stay with God and carry out our God-given purpose faithfully. God is calling us to be a part of this foolproof journey. He is Alpha and Omega who can effectively guide us because He knows the end from the beginning.

So, as we turn the final pages of "Foolproof," let us not merely see it as the end of a book but as the beginning of an empowered journey. Let this message resonate deeply within us as we step out into the world, armed with the profound wisdom and guidance offered within these pages. Our lives become a testament to the transformative power of faith, hope, and the unwavering light of divine guidance.

Made in the USA
Middletown, DE
25 September 2023

39108950R00135